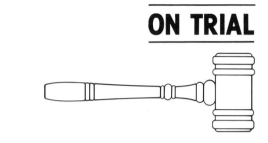

ON TRIAL

FAMOUS
SUPREME
COURT
CASES

ANDREW DAVID

Lerner Publications Company ▪ Minneapolis

ACKNOWLEDGMENTS: The illustrations are reproduced through the courtesy of: pp. 4, 7, Supreme Court Historical Society; pp. 8, 10, 25, 38 (left and right), 71, 114, 116, Library of Congress; p. 11 (left), Amherst College; p. 11 (right), Bowdoin College Museum of Art; pp. 14, 17, 20, 23, 47, 83, 84, 105, 112, United Press International, Inc.; pp. 22, 26, 27, 49, 54 (left and right), 58, 94, 98, 110, Wide World Photos; pp. 31, 36 (bottom), U.S. Army Photograph; pp. 33, 35 (top and bottom), 36 (top), War Relocation Authority, National Archives; p. 44, National Association for the Advancement of Colored People; pp. 79, 93, National Archives Gift Collection; p. 66, *Minnesota Daily;* p. 72, Religious News Service Photo; p. 80, *Chicago Sun-Times;* p. 91, Harris and Ewing; p. 96, Office of War Information, National Archives.

Cover art by Bob Klein

Chapter 10, *Allen Bakke: Affirmative Action*, was written by Dan Cohen.

LIBRARY OF CONGRESS CATALOGING IN PUBLICATION DATA

David, Andrew.
   Famous Supreme Court cases.

   (On Trial)
   Includes index.
   SUMMARY: Discusses ten landmark Supreme Court cases which addressed such constitutional issues as pretrial rights, the desegregation of schools, and the rights of juveniles.

   1. United States — Constitutional law — Cases — Juvenile literature. 2. Civil rights — United States — Cases — Juvenile literature. [1. United States — Constitutional law. 2. Civil rights. 3. United States. Supreme Court] I. Title. II. Series.

   KF4550.Z9W48   342'.73'085   79-16579
   ISBN 0-8225-1426-5

Manufactured in the United States of America. Published simultaneously in Canada by J.M. Dent & Sons (Canada) Ltd., Don Mills, Ontario.

International Standard Book Number: 0-8225-1426-5 Library of Congress Catalog Card Number: 79-16579

2   3   4   5   6   7   8   9   10   85   84   83   82   81

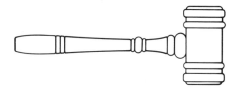

Contents

The courtroom of the Supreme Court Building in Washington, D.C.

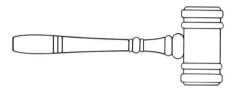

Introduction

The Supreme Court is the most powerful and most important unit in the part of the United States government known as the *judicial branch,* one of the three main divisions of the government. The other two branches are the *executive* and the *legislative;* the powers, duties, and limits of all three branches were established and defined by the founding fathers in the United States Constitution.

Article III of the Constitution begins: "The judicial power of the United States shall be vested in one Supreme Court, and in such inferior courts as the Congress may from time to time ordain and establish." By means of these words, the Supreme Court was established as the highest court in the country. It is first among all the *federal* courts; that is, courts that are involved with laws on the federal, or national, level. Today there are also 50 separate *state* court systems, which are concerned with their own individual state laws. The state courts have no connection with the federal courts, but the paths of these two court systems can cross at the Supreme Court level if there is a question of any violation of the U.S. Constitution in a state court case.

The Supreme Court is the guardian of the Constitution, which is the supreme law of the United States. The Court is responsible for interpreting and upholding all articles and amendments of the Constitution. It has sweeping power to overrule an act of Congress, an order of the president, or any state law if it finds that the act, order, or law violates some part of the Constitution.

Article III of the Constitution also defines the kinds of cases that can be tried before the Supreme Court. The Court can hear original cases only if they involve ambassadors or foreign representatives, or if one of the states of the union is a party to the case. The Supreme Court also can hear cases that have originated in lower courts, either federal or state. It hears such cases "on appeal"; that is, if a case is tried and decided in a lower court and one of the parties is not satisfied with the decision, that party can appeal the decision to a higher court. An appeal can be continued, each time to a higher court, until the case reaches the Supreme Court. This is the last stop in the appeals procedure because the ruling of the Court is final.

The great majority of cases heard and ruled on by the Supreme Court are those that have worked their way up the ladder of appeals. The Court hears many cases each year and rules on important issues and points of law that often have far-reaching effects on all people in the United States.

Today the Supreme Court is composed of nine persons, a chief justice and eight associate justices, each appointed

The justices of the United States Supreme Court in 1979: *(seated, left to right)* Byron R. White, William J. Brennan, Jr., Chief Justice Warren E. Burger, Potter Stewart, and Thurgood Marshall; *(standing, left to right),* W. H. Rehnquist, Harry A. Blackmun, Lewis F. Powell, Jr., and John P. Stevens.

by the president and approved by the Senate. The justices are appointed for life and cannot be removed except by impeachment. Appointment to the Supreme Court is perhaps the highest honor that a lawyer in the United States can achieve. Among the many fine and dedicated persons who have served on the Supreme Court have been John Jay, John Marshall, Oliver Wendell Holmes, Charles Evans Hughes, Louis Brandeis, William Howard Taft, and Earl Warren.

The Supreme Court does its work in a magnificent building, complete with Greek pillars and classic sculpture, in Washington, D.C., just a short walk from the

The Supreme Court Building was designed by architect Cass Gilbert and completed in 1935.

United States Capitol. It is an impressive and appropriate setting for such an important branch of the government.

In the early days of our country's history, however, the Supreme Court was not quite so important. At the end of the 1700s, there was no grand Supreme Court building in Washington; in fact, the Court did not even have a permanent place to meet in the nation's capital. During this period, an appointment to the Supreme Court was not considered the high honor that it is today, and it was often difficult to get qualified people to serve as justices. In addition to their duties in Washington, the Supreme Court justices were each responsible for a specific "circuit," or area, of what was then the United States. They had to spend a good part of each year traveling around their circuits, listening to cases in different cities and towns.

In these early years of the nation's history, the executive and legislative branches of government did not want a strong, or even equal, judicial branch, despite what was stated in the Constitution. Then John Marshall came on the scene. Marshall was secretary of state in 1801 when President John Adams appointed him chief justice of the Court. Marshall, unlike the president and Congress, believed in a strong system of courts. He felt that it was important for the judicial branch to use the powers that had been established for it by the Constitution.

In the same year of Marshall's appointment as chief justice, Thomas Jefferson became president. And in that year, Marshall confronted Jefferson's executive branch as well as the legislative branch of government in a case that would eventually determine the place of the judicial branch in the overall scheme of the United States government. It was the case of *William Marbury* v. *James Madison.*

William Marbury claimed that he had been appointed a justice of the peace by former president John Adams but that the official written appointment had not been delivered by the new president, Thomas Jefferson. Therefore, Marbury asked the Supreme Court to demand that his lawful appointment be delivered, according to form, by the secretary of state, James Madison. He made his appeal to the Court under a provision of a judiciary act passed by Congress in 1789.

Both Thomas Jefferson and the Congress in session

John Marshall

James Madison   Thomas Jefferson

were strongly opposed to the Court having the power to demand anything of either the executive or the legislative branch in any situation. In order to prevent the Supreme Court from considering Marbury's case, Congress went so far as to pass a law forbidding the Court to meet for a full year. But as soon as that year was up, Marshall brought the case back before the Court. If he had not, it would have been an admission that the Supreme Court did not have the power to uphold the law.

So the case of *Marbury* v. *Madison* was finally heard. When John Marshall announced the Court's decision, the situation took a surprising turn. Instead of declaring in favor of Marbury and his claim, Marshall said that the Supreme Court did not have the authority to pass judgment on the case. The provision of the Judiciary Act of 1789 that had allowed Marbury to bring his case to the

Court was, in fact, *unconstitutional.* The Court could only hear cases that were either tried in lower courts first or cases that involved a state or representatives of a foreign country. Marbury was in the wrong court; the Supreme Court could not rule on his particular case. But it *could* rule that the congressional law in question was unconstitutional and, therefore, void. And that is exactly what it did.

Marshall's handling of the case of *Marbury* v. *Madison* established the fact that the Court had the power to overrule any law passed by Congress if that law could be interpreted as unconstitutional. This general power of *judicial review* became very important in the history of the Court. It allowed the Supreme Court to play an active role in defending the constitutional rights of individual citizens. Because of the efforts of Chief Justice John Marshall, the United States gained a strong judicial branch of government.

Since the days of John Marshall, the Supreme Court has dealt with a wide variety of cases. In recent times, they have ranged from the case of Linda Brown, the young black girl who did not want to go to a segregated school, to the cases of Danny Escobedo and Ernesto Miranda, who had been found guilty of crimes in trials that they believed to be unfair. The cases themselves are usually brought to the attention of the Supreme Court by brilliant lawyers, but they can also reach the Court through the simple efforts of uneducated individuals like Clarence Gideon. These cases and the others described in this book have one thing in common: they deal with the constitutional rights of individuals and the body that guards those rights, the Supreme Court of the United States.

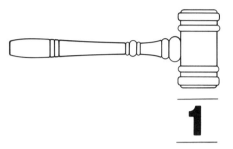

THE SCOTTSBORO NINE
The Right to a Fair Trial

A trial was going on in the small town of Scottsboro, Alabama, in April 1931, and there was not an empty seat in the courtroom.

Outside, National Guard troops were on duty around the courthouse doors and at other key places. The guardsmen looked out at a crowd of thousands of men, women, and children. Some of those people had traveled as much as 100 miles to be a part of the noisy crowd. Music and announcements blared out from loudspeakers, and the whole atmosphere seemed more like that of a state fair than of a legal proceeding.

Inside the courtroom, however, everyone was deadly serious. Nine youths, all black and ranging in age from 12 to 19, were on trial for their lives. Witnesses for both the prosecution and for the defense had testified, and the trial was winding down to its close, a verdict from the jury.

A lawyer summing up the case for the prosecution looked directly at the jury and said bitterly, "Guilty or

The Scottsboro Nine: *(from left to right)*, Ozie Powell, Clarence Norris, Charley Weems, Olen Montgomery, Roy Wright, Willie Roberson, Haywood Patterson, Andrew Wright, and Eugene Williams.

not guilty, let's get rid of these niggers."

In some ways the nine accused youths could probably consider themselves lucky just to be in that courtroom and on trial. The year was 1931, in the middle of a great depression. The place was in the poverty-stricken rural South where black people were generally hated. The nine youths were accused of raping two white girls, perhaps the most horrid of crimes in the mind of the average white southerner at that time. All those things combined to create the setting for a very dangerous situation. Lynching as an unofficial "punishment" of blacks accused of crimes against white people and their property was not uncommon in the South during those days. The armed national guardsmen surrounding the courthouse were grim reminders of the possibility of violent mob action.

Although the guardsmen were there to protect the nine black youths from a lynch mob during the trial, the *kind* of trial that they would get could not be guaranteed by military force. The right to a fair trial is supposedly guaranteed by the United States Constitution, but minority groups and the poor have sometimes been deprived of that right in one way or another. The Scottsboro Boys, as the nine came to be called, fell into that unfortunate category. Their case was to become one of the truly disgraceful examples of an unfair trial in American history.

The story of the Scottsboro Boys began in March 1931. At that time, hoboes and other unemployed wanderers were a common sight all over the country. There were so many that the railroads all but gave up trying to keep them from hitching rides on freight trains. A freight train traveling through northern Alabama had its share of these nonpaying passengers, and at one point a fight broke out in a boxcar between some white youths and a group of young blacks. The blacks won the fight and forced the white youths off the moving train. But the whites complained to a local stationmaster and said they wanted to file legal charges for assault. The stationmaster wired ahead to a local sheriff with information about the complaint.

When the train pulled into the small town of Paint Rock, Alabama, it was met by a large group of armed men. Most had been hurriedly "deputized" — designated as sheriff's officers — while they were waiting for the train. They swarmed onto the freight train and began going through it, boxcar by boxcar. When they finished, nine black boys, a white boy, and two white girls, all dressed in dingy coveralls and work clothes, had been taken off.

The three white youths were left to themselves. But a deputy sheriff saw to it that the nine blacks were roped together and loaded on a truck to be taken into Scottsboro. As the truck was about to leave, one of the white girls approached a deputy sheriff and calmly told him that she and her friend had been raped by the black youths. All the deputies standing near the truck were first stunned, and then enraged. Fortunately, some common sense prevailed, and the truck started off to Scottsboro with its nine prisoners. The deputy sheriff in charge realized that he had a very explosive case to handle. He put the two girls in a car, and they also headed into Scottsboro.

Once there, the girls were sent to a doctor to be examined, and word spread through the town about the supposed rape. The Scottsboro nine were locked up in the jail, and the sheriff and his deputies settled down to see how the people would react. By nightfall, several hundred people had gathered in front of the jail, and their mood was far from calm. The situation soon became difficult to control — lynching was a real possibility. From behind the barricaded doors, the sheriff called the governor of Alabama and asked for National Guard troops to protect the nine prisoners and help keep order.

Still under the protection of a National Guard, the nine black youths — Haywood Patterson, Olen Montgomery, Charley Weems, Clarence Norris, Willie Roberson, Ozie Powell, Eugene Williams, and Roy and Andrew Wright — eventually went on trial. All were to be represented by a public defender from Chattanooga, Tennessee. But, as one.

Members of the National Guard escort the Scottsboro defendants to their trial.

writer observed, this lawyer's "modest legal abilities were further limited by his inability to remain sober." (Dan T. Carter, *Scottsboro, A Tragedy of the American South.*)

When the case was brought to trial, the two girls who had been on the train, Victoria Price and Ruby Bates, went to the witness stand and described in detail how they had been ravished. There were, however, many contradictions in what they said. Moreover, statements by the two doctors who had examined the girls did not back up their claim that each had been raped six times. Another fact brought out in court was that one of the accused men was so painfully disabled by venereal disease that it would have been almost impossible for him to have committed the act.

In such a trial in the South at that time, however, a verdict of "guilty" was surely predictable and not long in coming. Eight of the nine were found guilty and sentenced to death. One, Roy Wright, also was found guilty, but because he was just 12 years old, the prosecution asked that he only be given a life sentence. Still, seven members of the jury refused to accept any sentence less than death, so a mistrial was called in the case of the 12-year-old.

The white citizens of Scottsboro and the surrounding countryside were satisfied; they had "gotten those niggers," guilty or not guilty. Surprisingly, however, protests began coming into Alabama from people not only in all parts of the United States but also in foreign countries. Individuals, organizations, and institutions claimed that justice had not been done. They demanded new trials and, this time, they insisted, *fair* trials. In Alabama, the reaction to these protests could only be described as puzzlement. "What's all the fuss about?" was the question Alabamans were asking.

When the time came for an appeal of the case, the International Labor Defense (ILD), which was a branch of the Communist Party in the United States, and the National Association for the Advancement of Colored People (NAACP) fought over which organization would represent the Scottsboro nine. The ILD won out and appealed to the Alabama Supreme Court in early 1932. But the appeal was rejected.

The ILD then took the case of the Scottsboro nine to the United States Supreme Court. The organization's lawyers claimed that the nine boys, on trial in a capital punishment case, had not been granted a fair trial and had not been represented by a good lawyer. In addition, they argued that the conduct of the trial could be considered unconstitutional because blacks were automatically kept off all Alabama juries. The Court agreed to review the case, but only on the subject of the defendants' right to counsel.

In its majority opinion, the Supreme Court held that the Constitution did guarantee the right to counsel in state proceedings where capital punishment could be the sentence. The 14th Amendment, the Court noted, provided that a state "shall not deprive any person of life, liberty, or property without due process of law. . . ." The Court ruled that the lawyer obtained for the Scottsboro nine had not been adequate for such a case, and because of that, the defendants had in effect been deprived of their right to "due process of the law." The Court then ordered new trials.

The Scottsboro nine would not all be tried together this time. They would be tried in small groups in four separate trials. But the first of the four trials would tell the story. Verdicts in the other trials would be predictable after the first verdict was in.

The ILD obtained Samuel Leibowitz, probably the finest criminal lawyer in New York at that time, to defend the nine young men. Leibowitz agreed to take their case free of charge, but demanded it be known that his taking the case in no way meant that he subscribed to the social or political views of the ILD. He said that the case was basically one of human rights, and that he was undertaking the defense only because of his commitment to these rights.

The new trials were scheduled to take place at Decatur, Alabama, under a new judge, James E. Horton. The time

A crowd gathers outside the court building in Decatur, Alabama.

was set for March 1933, two years after the alleged rape incident. Samuel Leibowitz, the defense lawyer, was clever and intelligent, well known for his dramatic courtroom performances and for the power of his relentless cross-examination of witnesses. From the beginning, he felt that there was one major issue in the Scottsboro case that would eventually have to be settled. Because black people were kept off jury lists in Alabama, they therefore would never be called to sit on a jury. Leibowitz believed this was unconstitutional and, more appropriate to his present task, grounds for appeal if he lost the Scottsboro case in Alabama. He emphasized this point in the selection of a jury, even though he knew no blacks would be allowed on the jury.

The main witness of the prosecution was once again Victoria Price, the young woman who, at the first trial, had been presented not only as an innocent victim of a horrible crime but also as a proud example of white southern womanhood. Again, she told the story of how she and Ruby Bates had been assaulted on that fateful day some two years earlier. Leibowitz succeeded in bringing out the contradictions and errors in her testimony, even though Victoria Price was a determined and stubborn witness who was not easily rattled by his questions.

Leibowitz then presented evidence in court that Miss Price and her friend Ruby Bates were not quite the pure blossoms of southern womanhood that the prosecution had pictured them to be. Instead, they had been prostitutes who had bestowed their favors for money on white and black men alike. Victoria Price had, in fact, been jailed in Huntsville, Alabama, for the crime of adultery.

There was no question in this second trial about whether the Scottsboro nine were receiving adequate counsel. They were, in truth, receiving the best defense available. Leibowitz went after each witness until the story was told straight and understandably; he even showed some witnesses to be outright liars by proving that their "eyewitness" testimony was physically impossible. He methodically chipped away piece by piece at the prosecution's case, but he was saving his blockbuster until the end.

As his last witness for the defense, Leibowitz brought into court the other alleged victim, Ruby Bates.

"Did any rape take place on the Chattanooga-to-Huntsville freight train on the day in question?" he asked.

Judge James E. Horton *(left)* listens to the testimony of a physician who examined Victoria Price.

"No. Not that I know of," was her answer.

When she was asked if there was somehow a possibility that Victoria Price might have been raped, she replied, "No. I was with her the whole time."

Her testimony was indeed startling, but Ruby Bates was not much better on the witness stand than her former friend. Again there were contradictions, and there were certainly some questions as to whether she had been influenced, or even bribed, to change her testimony. Ruby did not come off as a thoroughly believable witness.

After Ruby Bates' testimony, the trial, for all practical purposes, seemed to be over. The case presented to the

Defense attorney Samuel Leibowitz addresses the court.

jury did not appear to come even close to establishing "guilt beyond a reasonable doubt." Leibowitz was stunned as he listened to a member of the prosecution summing up their case. The lawyer for the prosecution pointed directly at Leibowitz and another lawyer at the defense table but kept his eyes on the jury as he said, "Show them that Alabama justice cannot be bought and sold with Jew money from New York."

Leibowitz objected strongly to such an ethnic slur in the court, but it did no good. He realized suddenly and correctly that the case would not be decided on the evidence that had been presented.

The case was finally turned over to the jurors, who after a short while returned their verdict: "Guilty as charged . . . the punishment, death in the electric chair."

Judge Horton, a man of honor and integrity, was appalled at the verdict. Later, after much thought, he announced that because the jury had reached a verdict so contrary to the evidence in the case, he was throwing out the jury's decision and called for a new trial. It was a brave act and a costly one. Judge Horton was voted out of office shortly afterwards, mainly because of that decision.

The trials went on, now with a new judge who quite clearly was partial toward the prosecution. At the end of one trial he instructed the jury on how to reach a "guilty" verdict, but "forgot" to tell them how to arrive at a "not guilty" verdict. The findings in the new trials continued to be "guilty" and the sentence, death.

Leibowitz appealed, taking the case up to the United States Supreme Court again. There he argued that the state of Alabama consistently kept blacks from sitting as jurors by never placing their names on the lists from which jury members were drawn.

In April 1935, the United States Supreme Court reached an historic decision. Chief Justice Charles Evans Hughes wrote the majority opinion in which he pointed out that by excluding blacks from juries, the state in effect denied a black defendant the "equal protection of the laws" as required under the 14th Amendment. The Court's ruling put an end to this form of discrimination by opening jury service to all citizens. It also overturned the verdicts against the Scottsboro nine and ordered new trials to be held.

Back to the Alabama courts they went. Over the next

Charles Evans Hughes

two years new trials were held, new verdicts of guilty were found, and new appeals were drawn up. More important, however, serious behind-the-scenes bargaining was going on between the defense and the prosecution. Both sides wanted to end this seemingly endless case. Finally, in 1937, more than six years since the time of the alleged crime, both sides agreed to a compromise plan that would once and forever end the trials. Four of the defendants — Olen Montgomery, Willie Roberson, Eugene Williams, and Roy Wright — were to be released immediately. The remaining five were to go to jail but were to be paroled quietly sometime before the next year was over.

Alabama state officials, however, did not follow through on the agreement and did not release the five. It was not

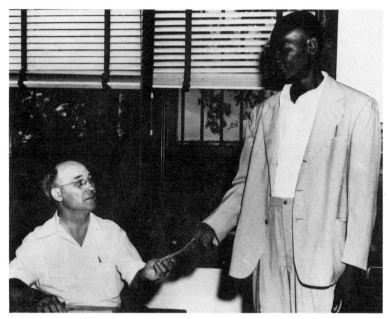

Andrew Wright receives $13.45 in "go free" pay on his release from prison in June 1950.

until six years later that three of the others — Charley Weems, Clarence Norris, and Andrew Wright — were freed. They were refused permission to leave the state, and when Wright did leave, he was put back in jail. Ozie Powell was released in 1946, and in 1948 Haywood Patterson escaped. Finally, in 1950, the last of the Scottsboro nine, Andrew Wright, was released after serving a total of 19 years in prison.

The Supreme Court had made two important decisions as a result of the Scottsboro trials — one guaranteeing a defendant's right to counsel and the other preventing states from excluding blacks from juries because of race. The Court by its actions contributed to saving the lives of the Scottsboro nine, even though it did not keep them

Clarence Norris, October 1976

from spending many years in jail.

The trials of the Scottsboro nine were a sad commentary on the injustices that can exist within the judicial system. They were a legal disgrace, and they were never justly resolved. It was not until 1976 that the state of Alabama finally made some effort to redress the wrongs done to the Scottsboro nine. In that year, Clarence Norris, the last of the nine known to be still alive, was granted a full pardon by the state, on the grounds that there was proof of his innocence. After receiving the pardon, the 64-year-old Norris told reporters that he felt no malice toward anyone even though "I do feel bad . . . because I was accused wrong." The pardon had come 45 years too late for this victim of legal injustice.

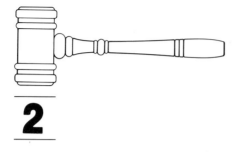

2

FRED KOREMATSU
Relocating American Citizens in Wartime

In many countries people have been imprisoned, even executed, without having committed a real crime. In Nazi Germany, being a Jew, a gypsy, or a member of any group considered "undesirable" was reason enough to be sent to a concentration camp or a death chamber. During certain periods in the history of the USSR, Russians whose political ideas were not in line with those of the government were often sent to Siberian labor camps or, according to a common joke, were "lucky" enough to be confined to mental institutions. Even in the United States, as we now remember with regret, human beings were once held in bondage as slaves.

Traditionally, Americans have thought of prisons, reform schools, and juvenile homes as places to confine only those persons lawfully convicted of crimes. Prisoner-of-war camps have been considered places to keep enemy soldiers so that they could no longer fight against American forces. Most citizens of the United States do not like to think that people in this country could be imprisoned or confined because of their political ideas or racial backgrounds, or for any reason other than being found guilty of a crime. The ideal is a noble one, but in cold reality it has not always been upheld. We have only to look at the historical record during World War II to learn this unpleasant truth.

When the United States declared war on Japan in 1941 after the attack on Pearl Harbor, there were approximately 125,000 people of Japanese ancestry living in this country. Most of them — about 112,000 — lived on the West Coast; in this group was a young man named Fred Korematsu, who lived in Oakland, California, with his parents and three brothers. Korematsu was a *nisei* (NEE-say), the term for a Japanese person born in the United States. Just like 70,000 other Japanese-Americans, he was a citizen by birth.

Like many immigrants in the United States, the Japanese lived together in their own neighborhoods or small communities. The older immigrants were reluctant to give up many of their Japanese customs, and for the most part worked and socialized only among themselves. The American-born nisei, however, did not cling to ancestral tradition. They quickly accepted and were absorbed into the American way of life.

Fred Korematsu's youth was very much like that of any ordinary young American growing up in the peaceful but difficult years before the war. English was his "native" language, and he went to average American public schools. He played and followed American sports, hung around with his classmates — white and Japanese alike — at a neighborhood drugstore, listened to the same music and radio programs, and dressed in the same style clothes as his white friends. There was never a reason for Fred Korematsu to question his rights as an American citizen. These constitutionally guaranteed rights were always there — so he took them for granted. But the Japanese assault on Pearl Harbor on December 7, 1941, changed that with a devastating suddenness.

Not surprisingly, the American people were outraged at the attack and expressed their feelings toward the Japanese nation with bitterness and hatred. For the Japanese-Americans in the United States, a change took place almost overnight. They became "Japs," and were looked on as an extension of the enemy. There was suspicion about their loyalty to America, and there was a growing fear that all Japanese were spies or saboteurs. The comfortable life that Japanese people had come to know in America became a nightmare. They were denied food and service in stores. Banks refused to release their money or honor their checks. They were insulted and ridiculed in the streets, and some were even attacked and beaten.

The climax of this attitude came in February 1942, three months after the bombing of Pearl Harbor. The commander of American military defenses on the West Coast, Lieutenant General John L. DeWitt, requested that all 112,000 Japanese-Americans in the area be evacuated and "relocated" somewhere away from the Pacific coast. General DeWitt explained that there was a possibility of a Japanese invasion of the western United States. Because no one really knew which side the Japanese-Americans favored, it was a military necessity to remove them — imperative, the general said, if the United States was to defend its western coast successfully.

Lieutenant General John L. DeWitt, commander of American military defenses on the West Coast

Officials in Washington, D.C., at first were skeptical of General DeWitt's proposal. After all, taking a large group of people, most of them American citizens, from their homes and sending them to relocation camps had never been done before in the United States. Moreover, no one was demanding that German-Americans and Italian-Americans be removed from the East Coast, though the United States was also at war with Germany and Italy. It appeared to some that the idea of moving the Japanese was based more on "racial" factors than on military need. Although General DeWitt had claimed the evacuation was necessary for military reasons, he revealed other feelings in testimony before a Congressional committee when he said, "A Jap's a Jap. It makes no difference whether he's an American or not."

But as the success of the Japanese military actions increased in the days immediately after Pearl Harbor, so did the nation's resentment of the Japanese-Americans. Newspaper and radio reports fueled the fear that the West Coast might be attacked. In Washington, the highly respected columnist Walter Lippmann reflected popular attitudes when he wrote: "I understand fully and appreciate thoroughly the unwillingness of Washington to adopt a policy of mass evacuation and mass internment of all those who are technically enemy aliens. . . . However, the Pacific Coast is officially a combat zone: some part of it may at any moment be a battlefield. Nobody's constitutional rights include the right to reside and do business on a battlefield." The "nobody," of course, referred only to Japanese-Americans.

Finally, President Franklin D. Roosevelt gave in to the pressure from General DeWitt, the news media, and other groups that wanted the Japanese moved away from the West Coast. He issued an order that authorized the Department of War to designate certain parts of the country as war zones "from which any or all persons may be excluded."

At first, General DeWitt only ordered a curfew for the Japanese-Americans, which required them to remain in their homes between eight o'clock at night and six o'clock in the morning. Later, the Japanese-Americans were asked to relocate voluntarily in inland areas. Only about 7 out of every 100, however, were willing to give up their homes and jobs. Those who did agree to relocate

Japanese-American families waiting to be evacuated from San Francisco in April 1942

did not receive a very warm welcome in the areas to which they moved. Governor Chase Clark of Idaho announced, "The Japs live like rats, breed like rats, and act like rats. I don't want them coming into Idaho. . . ." Newspapers and officials in other states expressed equally harsh feelings.

When most of the Japanese-Americans did not leave the West Coast voluntarily, General DeWitt issued the final order to move out *all* of them. The War Relocation Agency was established hastily to build camps and supervise all phases of the evacuation as well as the daily operations within the camps. As soon as the order went out, the people to be relocated were given 48 hours to dispose of their homes and all other property that they could not carry with them. They were sent to assembly centers for processing and then to the relocation camps. Living conditions in the camps were very poor. Workers, some of whom had held good and prosperous jobs before, were paid from $12 per month for unskilled laborers to $19 per month for professionals such as doctors and lawyers. In other parts of the country German prisoners of war, who had fought against the United States, been captured, and brought to prison camps in the United States, were paid slightly more than $20 per month for their work.

Fred Korematsu decided immediately that he did not want to be interned in a relocation camp. He was 22 years old at the time and had a non-Japanese girlfriend whom he did not want to leave. He felt it was unjust and even illegal that he was to be forced into an internment camp. After all, he was a native-born American citizen, and his loyalties were firmly on the side of the United States. (He had even tried to enlist in the U.S. Army after the attack on Pearl Harbor but was not accepted.)

Because of his strong feelings, Fred Korematsu ignored the relocation order and went into hiding. When confronted by anyone asking about his nationality, he claimed to be Chinese. His pretense did not work, however. Eventually he was arrested and brought to trial for having violated the evacuation order. The American Civil Liberties Union defended Korematsu in court, but the case was lost. Korematsu received five years probation and was sent off to an internment camp at Topaz, Utah.

After this initial defeat, Korematsu's lawyers appealed his case, step by step, all the way to the Supreme Court. Their argument was based on the grounds that it was unconstitutional to take people out of their homes and

Japanese-Americans on their way to internment camps

Occupants of relocation camps were housed in barracks like the ones pictured above. Many of the camps were located in desert regions of western states; below is an aerial view of a camp near Parker, Arizona.

put them in internment camps solely on the basis of their race. It was noted that other so-called "enemy aliens" had not been relocated. The lawyers held that there was no evidence that Korematsu was in any way disloyal. In addition, as an American citizen he had a constitutionally guaranteed right to be treated as an individual and not as a member of a particular racial group.

The lawyers for the government argued that Fred Korematsu and the 112,000 other Japanese-Americans were interned under a lawful military order issued for the protection of America's West Coast. The government lawyers pointed out that it had been proven that certain Japanese-Americans were loyal to Japan and therefore a threat to the war efforts. Because it could not be determined just which Japanese might be disloyal to America, it became a military necessity to remove all Japanese-Americans from a "war zone."

The Supreme Court did not announce its decision until December 18, 1944, more than two and half years after the original evacuation order. The decision went against Fred Korematsu: six justices upheld the military order, and three voted against it. Justice Hugo L. Black wrote the majority opinion, in which he said:

> The military authorities, charged with the primary responsibility of defending our shores, concluded that curfew provided inadequate protection and ordered exclusion. . . . Korematsu was not excluded from the military area because of hostility to him or his race. He was excluded because we were at war with the Japanese Empire, because the properly constituted military authorities feared an invasion of our west

Hugo Black

Frank Murphy

coast and felt constrained to take proper security measures. . . ."

Disagreeing completely with Justice Black's opinion, Justice Frank Murphy wrote a dissenting opinon and referred to the case as an instance of "obvious racial discrimination." Justice Murphy pointed out that loyalty hearings should have been held to determine whether there was a cause to remove *individual* Japanese-Americans. Those whose loyalty was doubtful should then be removed. But mass evacuation, he said, was in violation of the constitutional rights to "due process of law."

Fred Korematsu lost his case. His conviction was upheld by the Supreme Court despite the strong arguments of Justice Murphy. Perhaps it was because of the times:

the United States was still at war with Japan, and the major civil rights issues that would find their way to the Supreme Court in the 1960s were not among the major concerns of that day. As for Fred Korematsu, his case was actually being resolved outside the courts, because the War Relocation Agency had already begun a program to do away with the camps and to help the people confined in them to re-enter American society. Officials of the agency and other decision-makers in Washington had realized there was really no need for the camps.

Justice Murphy may have been outvoted in the Korematsu case, but in his written opinion he left a powerful statement about the basic human and civil rights guaranteed by the Constitution — a guide, perhaps, for later Supreme Courts that would face decisions on the many aspects of civil rights. He said: "Racial discrimination in any form and in any degree has no justifiable part whatever in our democratic way of life. . . . All residents of this nation are kin in some way by blood or culture to a foreign land. Yet they are primarily and necessarily a part of the new and distinct civilization of the United States. They must accordingly be treated at all times as the heirs of the American experiment and as entitled to all the rights and freedoms guaranteed by the Constitution."

Because of the decision in the Korematsu case and the fact that the Court has not had occasion to reconsider it, the government still has the power to "relocate" or intern entire racial groups for reasons of military necessity or national emergency. Let us hope that the situation in which this power would be exercised will never rise again. But if it does, may that power be exercised only for grave need and not for racial or political motives.

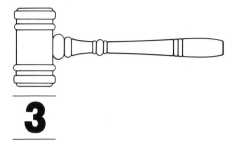

3

LINDA BROWN
Desegregation of Public Schools

Washington, D.C., the nation's capital, is a city filled with monuments honoring great American leaders of the past. In this famous city are kept the originals of the most important documents in American history: the Declaration of Independence and the Constitution, including the Bill of Rights. Washington is also the place where the president of the United States lives and works and where Congress and the Supreme Court meet. The city itself has a reputation as the greatest center of democracy in the world.

In this historic city, on a warm September day in 1950, a small group of adults and youngsters entered one of Washington's junior high schools. The purpose of their visit was to enroll the children in school. But the principal told them that she did not have authority to register *those* children in *that* school. It was a school for whites only, and the youngsters were black.

The group then went to the board of education offices.

There the superintendent of schools told them that the laws of Washington, D.C., required separate schools for blacks and whites. He explained that this was the federal law — created by Congress, no less. Because Washington, D.C., is not a state and is not in any state, it is governed by federal laws made by Congress. The superintendent said he could not do anything to help the black children attend an all-white school. Their only hope would be in the courts, which is precisely where the parents then took their case. It became known as the "Spottswood Bolling case," because that was the name of one of the black youngsters seeking admission to the all-white school.

Topeka, Kansas, is a small city more than 1,000 miles from Washington and, from all outward appearances, very different in many ways. But in Topeka about the same time, a case similar to that of Spottswood Bolling was taking shape. Linda Brown, an 11-year-old black girl and the daughter of a minister, wanted to enter an all-white school. Because Topeka, like Washington, had a law permitting segregated schools, Linda Brown's request was turned down. Linda's parents decided to go to court and challenge that law.

Linda Brown and Spottswood Bolling were not the only ones confronting segregated school systems in the early 1950s. In Virginia, South Carolina, and Delaware, three more lawsuits were being started to challenge the segregation of black and white pupils in public schools. The battle that the challengers faced would not be an easy one, because segregated schools had a long history in the United States. From the time that the slaves were freed in 1863, separate schools for blacks and whites were common in the deep South, in the Southwest, and in the border states between the North and South. More than 90 years later, 17 states, as well as Washington, D.C., still had laws allowing separate schools for black pupils and white pupils. Linda Brown and Spottswood Bolling were only 2 among 2.5 million blacks and 8 million whites attending segregated schools.

Such schools were able to exist because it was legal at the time to have separate schools *if* they were equal. By providing *separate but equal facilities* for black and white students, states could claim that they were depriving no one of the constitutional right to an equal education.

The idea of "separate but equal" facilities was not merely a theory created by states that wanted to maintain segregated schools. It was supported by a United States Supreme Court decision made in 1896, more than half a century earlier. The decision resulted from a case called *Plessy* v. *Ferguson*. It involved transportation rather than education, but it laid a foundation for the belief that "separate but equal" facilities were legal under the United States Constitution. Plessy, a black man, was sent to jail in Louisiana for refusing to leave the "whites only" section of a train. The Supreme Court eventually heard the case and ruled that because the railroad provided equal facilities for blacks and whites, the rights of one race were not inferior to those of the other. Therefore, Plessy was wrong. His conviction was upheld, and the practice of segregation for racial reasons was given strong backing.

For more than 50 years after that, a number of states followed the tradition of "separate but equal" facilities, not only in public transportation and in schools but also in such places or facilities as stores, theaters, washrooms, and even drinking fountains for the public.

The issue that the lawyers for Linda Brown in Topeka, Kansas, and Spottswood Bolling in Washington, D.C., were taking to court was whether "separate" facilities were in fact equal. Their lawyers insisted that "separate" was not equal and, therefore, was not constitutional. In effect, they were suggesting that the Supreme Court had previously been wrong when it ruled in the *Plessy* v. *Ferguson* case.

Linda Brown lost her case in the District Court of Kansas, and Spottswood Bolling lost his case in Washington. The two similar lawsuits in South Carolina and Virginia were also lost. Those four cases were then appealed separately up the judicial ladder to the United States Supreme Court.

In Delaware, however, the fifth case concerning segregated schools was lost by the state. Delaware's supreme court held that "separate" was not equal. That state's attorney general also appealed the decision to the United States Supreme Court, but from the opposite side. And so, in 1952, the Supreme Court agreed to consider all five cases together.

Five teams of lawyers represented the black complainants. Each team was to argue the case for its own client before the Supreme Court. Among the brilliant and respected lawyers representing the complainants was Thurgood Marshall, a black man who had been associated with the National Association for the Advancement of Colored People (NAACP) for many years. During a remarkable career, Marshall was destined to argue more than 30 civil rights cases before the Supreme Court, to be named Solicitor General of the United States, and, in 1967, to be ap-

Thurgood Marshall

pointed by President Lyndon B. Johnson to the Supreme Court, the first of his race to achieve that position.

The arguments on both sides were long and detailed, because the decision that the Supreme Court would make could change the way of life for millions of American citizens, black and white alike. The complainants called for an end to segregated public facilities. Segregated facilities were unequal, they said, and refusing a person admission to a public school because he or she happened to be black was discrimination. It did not matter whether other "equal" facilities were available or not. The mere fact that a person was denied admittance to one school only because of race was *in itself* an act of segregation and therefore unconstitutional, under the provision of the

14th Amendment to the Constitution. This amendment stated that no state shall "deprive any person of life, liberty, or property without due process of law; nor deny to any person within its jurisdiction the equal protection of the laws."

On the other side, lawyers for the four states and Washington, D.C., argued that the Supreme Court had already ruled on this issue in the case of *Plessy* v. *Ferguson.* By so doing, the Court had clearly established that "separate but equal" facilities were constitutionally legal, those lawyers said. In addition, they pointed out that the United States Congress — the governmental body that had framed the 14th Amendment — had enacted a law that *required* a segregated school system in the nation's capital. After all, they asked, who could better interpret the meaning of the 14th Amendment than the branch of government that had originally authored it? Congress had in effect interpreted the meaning by enacting a law to permit segregated schools in Washington, D.C., according to this argument.

All five cases dragged on, but in mid-1953 they were interrupted by the death of the chief justice of the Court, Fred M. Vinson. President Dwight D. Eisenhower then appointed a new chief justice, Earl Warren, who in the succeeding years was to become one of the most famous and most controversial members of the Supreme Court.

By the end of 1953, the Court still had not reached a decision in the school segregation cases. Lawyers who had presented their cases were called back for further arguments, and other experts were brought in to add information that the justices felt was essential in reaching their decision.

In early 1954, the Court at last announced that it had made its rulings in those important cases. Two separate decisions would be read. The case involving Spottswood Bolling and Washington, D.C., would be treated separately because it involved only federal law and therefore could not be considered under the 14th Amendment, which concerns state regulations. The other four cases would be ruled on as one. This group of four cases would become known as *Brown* v. *Board of Education of Topeka, Kansas,* only because that particular case headed the list of four as published by the Court.

The Brown decision was the first to be read that Monday in 1954. The majority opinion was written by Chief Justice Earl Warren, and the majority in this case was unanimous.

Chief Justice Warren began: "In each of the cases, minors of the Negro race, through their legal representatives, seek the aid of the courts in obtaining admission to the public schools of their community on a non-segregated basis. . . . The plaintiffs contend that segregated public schools are not 'equal' and cannot be made 'equal,' and that hence they are deprived of the equal protection of the laws (*guaranteed by the 14th Amendment*)."

The chief justice then went on to consider what the authors of the 14th Amendment did intend in regard to public schools, if indeed they intended anything in particular. As part of the decision, the justices felt it was important to compare the function and value of education in the year 1954 with the much earlier period when the 14th Amendment was written.

Chief Justice Warren emphasized that everyone was entitled to an "equal" education. He summed up the

Three attorneys in the school segregation case — *(from left to right)*, George Hayes, Thurgood Marshall, and James Nabrit, Jr. — posed on the steps of the Supreme Court Building after the Court's decision was announced.

findings of the Court briefly but directly: "We come then to the question presented. Does segregation of children in public schools solely on the basis of race, even though the physical facilities and other 'tangible' factors may be equal, deprive the children of the minority group of equal educational opportunities? We believe that it does."

The Supreme Court's second ruling of the day, the case of Spottswood Bolling, was in favor of the complainant as well. It was based, however, on the "due process of law" provision of the 5th Amendment, which pertains only to federal law.

The Supreme Court realized that its school segregation decisions raised enormous difficulties for the states. Schools would have to be integrated on a fair basis. In some cases, new schools would have to be built to replace below-standard schools that black children had been forced to attend. The problems were many. The cases that had just been decided by the Court, Chief Justice Warren pointed out, would have to go back on the docket, that is, on the Supreme Court's calendar. The Court wanted further hearings and arguments so that it could make recommendations about the ways in which the new ruling should be carried out by the states.

It was more than a year before the Court finished its hearings and made its recommendations. It ordered the lower courts to maintain the responsibility of requiring local school districts and school boards to carry out the new law. The Court directed the lower courts to accomplish this "with all deliberate speed."

State courts did not all comply "with all deliberate speed," however, and 10 years were to pass before Congress would enact a strong civil rights law to force solutions to the problem. Yet even today the solutions have not been worked out completely. Problems still face all regions of the United States in achieving truly integrated schools.

Linda Brown, Spottswood Bolling, and all the other young people who were part of these cases have since grown up. But as youngsters in school they had played a major role in a Supreme Court decision of historic importance. Theirs was a major step forward in the effort to provide equal rights and equal opportunities for all people.

Ten years after the Supreme Court's decision, Linda Brown stood in front of the Topeka school to which she had been denied admission as a child.

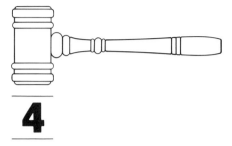

4

DOLLREE MAPP
Illegal Search and Seizure

The right to own property and to enjoy privacy within that property is usually taken for granted by the citizens of the United States. In fact, the Constitution guarantees that right, but this guarantee has not always been enforced. Unfortunately, there are countless legal "horror stories" on record — cases in which soldiers, police, or other law enforcement agents have broken into homes and buildings, searching without warrants and sometimes leaving everything in shambles or hauling people off to jail if anything incriminating was found.

Dollree Mapp had just that kind of experience. In 1957, she and her 15-year-old daughter were living on the second floor of a two-family house in Cleveland, Ohio. Mrs. Mapp was at home alone on the afternoon of May 23 when the doorbell rang. She went downstairs and saw three policemen at the door. One of them told Mrs. Mapp they had reason to believe that someone wanted by the police was hiding in the house.

Mrs. Mapp said she would have to talk to her lawyer before letting the police come in to search. She then phoned the lawyer, who told her: "Ask if they have a search warrant. If they say they do, make them let you see it. It'll be a legal-looking paper that says they are allowed to enter your house and search it. It should be signed by a judge. If they don't have a search warrant, you don't have to let them in."

Mrs. Mapp went back to the door and asked to see a warrant. The policemen looked at each other and then, with more than a trace of irritation, told her that they did not have one. She locked the downstairs door and the three policemen trudged back outside. One of them radioed the police station and explained what had happened. Then he joined his two partners in front of the entrance to the house.

The reason the police wanted to search the house was that they had received a tip that a fugitive was hiding there. Their informant also had told the police that there were gambling materials hidden in Mrs. Mapp's residence.

Mrs. Mapp became steadily more upset as she stared out of her upstairs window, keeping as close a watch on the three policemen as they were keeping on her house. A short while later, a police lieutenant telephoned Mrs. Mapp and told her to let his men come in and search the house. But she repeated what she had told the other policemen and then hung up. The police stayed outside, so Mrs. Mapp called her lawyer again. He told her that she shouldn't worry and that he would come right over. In the meantime, two squad cars pulled up with four more police officers, who got out and joined the three in front of the house.

All seven police officers demanded to be allowed to enter. Mrs. Mapp, talking to them from her second-story window, still refused. A short time later, she saw her lawyer's car pull up in front, and she started downstairs to let him in. She was stopped halfway down, however, by several policemen who had broken into the hallway. Outside, the other police officers stopped the lawyer from entering the house.

"Let me see your warrant," Mrs. Mapp said.

One of the policemen waved a piece of paper in front of her, saying "Don't worry. Here it is." When the officer did not hand the paper to her, Mrs. Mapp snatched it from his hand. The policemen demanded that she give it back, but Mrs. Mapp refused. Then, as the officer tried to grab the paper, she stuffed it down the front of her dress.

"Get that back," one of the other police officers shouted, and grabbed at Mrs. Mapp. She struggled, but he held her firmly while the first officer reached down into the front of her dress and pulled out the sheet of paper. "Now handcuff her," the officer said, as he put the paper into his pocket.

Several policemen led Mrs. Mapp upstairs to her bedroom where, handcuffed to one of the policemen, she was told to sit on the bed and not to bother anyone. The other policemen then searched her home, room by room. Outside, Mrs. Mapp's lawyer demanded to be let into the house, declaring that what the police were doing was against the law. The officers at first argued with him, but finally just ignored him.

When the entire second floor had been searched and nothing of interest was found, the police went down to the basement of the house. There they opened an old trunk, and inside it found some material — several pamphlets and a few photographs — that the policemen decided were obscene. They took the material as evidence and told Mrs. Mapp she was being placed under arrest for breaking a state law that forbade possession of obscene materials.

Mrs. Mapp protested that the whole thing was ridiculous. In the first place, she claimed, those things did not even belong to her. They were the property of a former tenant who had moved out of the house and had left the trunk and its contents. Mrs. Mapp also said that she and another woman had been planning to send the pamphlets and pictures to their rightful owner. The police informed Mrs. Mapp that a judge would have to decide on that matter. Their duty was simply to arrest her, not to determine her guilt or innocence. They took her to the police station and booked her on a charge of possessing obscene material.

In court Mrs. Mapp pleaded "not guilty" to the charge. During the trial, the prosecution did not produce a search warrant. In fact, there was no testimony that there ever had been a search warrant. But despite the way in which the evidence (the obscene material) was obtained, Mrs. Mapp was found guilty. She was sentenced to serve one to eight years in the Ohio state prison for women.

At this point, Mrs. Mapp and her lawyer appealed the case to the Ohio Supreme Court. The court decided in her favor, and by a bare majority of four to three ruled that the state obscenity law under which she was convicted was unconstitutional because it had deprived Mrs. Mapp of her basic rights. But there was another problem. According to Ohio statutes, the state supreme court could not overrule a law if more than one justice voted in favor of keeping it. In Mrs. Mapp's case, three justices had, in fact, voted to uphold the law. Therefore, the state supreme court could not change her conviction even though the majority of four justices thought that it was unconstitutional.

Mrs. Mapp then appealed to the United States Supreme Court. In 1961, four years after her conviction, the Court agreed to hear Mrs. Mapp's case. When the case came before the Court, her lawyer did not argue that Mrs. Mapp's rights had been denied by an illegal search and seizure. Instead, he based his case on the argument that the Ohio state law forbidding the possession of obscene materials was unconstitutional — the same point raised by the Ohio Supreme Court. The reason for this approach was simply that it offered a better chance for a reversal of Mrs. Mapp's conviction. The question of whether the constitutional protections against illegal searches and

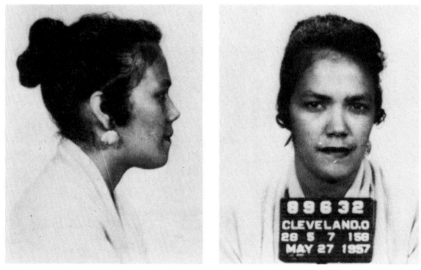

Dollree Mapp

seizures applied to state court proceedings was a much larger constitutional issue.

Despite the presentation of the case of Mrs. Mapp's lawyer, the Supreme Court decided to rule specifically on the subject of illegal searches and seizures. The legal question was in regard to a provision of the 4th Amendment to the Constitution — "the right of the people to be secure in their persons, houses, papers, and effects, against unreasonable searches and seizures." Did this provision apply to cases in state courts as well as federal courts? In the past, it had been ruled that the provision applied only in federal court cases. State courts could decide themselves whether materials obtained by illegal searches and seizures could be presented as evidence in their own courts.

Justice Thomas C. Clark wrote the majority opinion for himself and five other justices. Citing both the 4th Amendment and the 14th Amendment guarantee of "due process of law" and "equal protection of the laws" for *all* citizens, Justice Clark wrote: "We hold that all evidence obtained by searches and seizures in violation of the Constitution is, by the same authority, inadmissable in a state court."

By the Court's ruling, Mrs. Mapp was finally a free person, and the conviction against her was erased from the records. On a larger scale, the Supreme Court had guaranteed an important constitutional right to all persons by clearly and firmly protecting them against illegal searches and seizures.

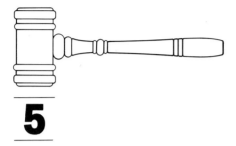

5

CLARENCE EARL GIDEON
The Right to Have a Lawyer

In April 1962, Clarence Earl Gideon sat in the Florida state prison writing a letter to the United States Supreme Court. He was not an educated man, and he worked hard on the letter, but he knew exactly what he wanted to say. "It makes no difference how old I am or what color I am or what church I belong to if any. The question is I did not get a fair trial. The question is very simple. I requested the court to appoint me [an] attorney and the court refused."

In those few short sentences, Clarence Earl Gideon summed up his problem very clearly, though he did not use the words that lawyers use. Because he could not afford to hire a lawyer, Gideon had asked the court to appoint one for him. The judge had refused, and Gideon went on trial, forced to defend himself on a charge of "breaking and entering."

Gideon knew that the 6th Amendment to the U.S. Constitution specifically provides that "in all criminal prosecutions, the accused shall enjoy the right . . . to have the assistance of counsel for his defense." But what he failed to understand was that the 6th Amendment only guaranteed the *right* to have a lawyer; it did not say that the courts were required to *provide* one for a particular person. In addition, the 6th Amendment itself did not guarantee that right in a *state* proceeding. If, in fact, the right was to be guaranteed in state courts, it would have to fall under the "due process" provision of the 14th Amendment.

Even so, it seems surprising that in 1962 a person could be put on trial for a crime without the benefit of a lawyer's help. Unfortunately, it was not an uncommon situation. At that time, the law only required courts to appoint lawyers for poor defendants in cases that might lead to the death penalty or cases in which defendants could not defend themselves for a serious reason, such as insanity.

This subject had been brought to the Supreme Court's attention before 1962. In fact, the Court had ruled on very much the same issue 20 years earlier. The case involved a farmer named Smith Betts who went to trial for robbery in Maryland. He asked the court to provide a lawyer, claiming he could not afford to hire one. The judge turned down the request. Betts appealed to the Supreme Court but he lost his case there as well.

In his prison cell in Florida, however, Clarence Earl Gideon apparently did not know about the Betts case. In fact, between 1942 and 1962 many states had ignored the Betts decision and had begun to provide lawyers in various criminal cases. At the time of Gideon's trial, 37 of the 50 states provided lawyers for poor defendants in all

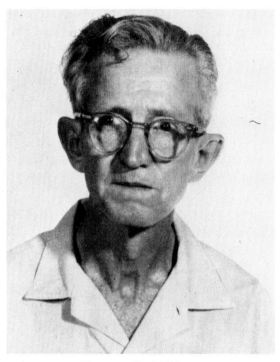

Clarence Earl Gideon

felony cases — that is, generally speaking, all those criminal cases in which the punishment could be one year's imprisonment or more. Eight other states *usually* provided lawyers for such cases. The other five states held to the practice of providing lawyers only in capital punishment cases. Unfortunately for Clarence Earl Gideon, Florida was one of those five.

In 1962, Gideon was 52 years old. His wrinkled face and his thin, bent body gave him the appearance of an old man. Life had not been good to him, and he showed it. And the way in which he conducted his life had been less than admirable. He knew that and admitted frankly in a letter about his past, "I will not be proud of this biography . . . ."

Gideon was born in 1910 in Hannibal, Missouri, the town on the Mississippi River that was Mark Twain's home and the setting for his books about Tom Sawyer and Huckleberry Finn. Gideon's childhood was unhappy. His father had died when Clarence was three years old. His mother was extremely strict, and the boy could not get along at all with his stepfather. So when he was 14 Clarence ran away, going as far as California. A year later he returned to Missouri but not to his home. Shortly afterwards he was arrested for stealing clothes from a store. When his mother learned of his arrest, she asked that he be sent to the state reform school. A year later he was released, but his reform school experience was only the beginning of what would become a lifelong series of entrances and exits from various jails.

At 18, he was sentenced to 10 years in the Missouri state prison for burglary. After three years he was paroled, but in another three years, at the age of 24, he was back in prison, this time at the federal penitentiary in Leavenworth, Kansas, for having burglarized a federal government armory. Three years later, he was outside, again for only three years. Once more Clarence Gideon was arrested in Missouri for burglary and sentenced to 10 years. After four years, however, Gideon escaped. He remained free for almost a year, then was recaptured and sent back to the state prison for six more years. That term ended in 1950, but a year later he was in a Texas state prison, serving a one-year term for burglary.

For nine years, from 1952 to 1961, Gideon stayed out of trouble with the law. He married his third wife, and they had two children, both boys. The couple also re-gained custody of the wife's three children by a previous marriage, and the family moved to Panama City, Florida, a dismal, poverty-ridden town on the northern coast of the Gulf of Mexico.

Gideon's next arrest occurred in an area called Bay Harbor, just outside Panama City. He was charged with breaking and entering a pool hall with the intent of steal-ing. Ironically, he could have gotten into that pool hall easily because he ran a poker game there for the owner. In court, Gideon staunchly claimed he was innocent and pleaded "not guilty" to the charge.

Gideon's trial in Panama City was before Judge Robert L. McCrary and a jury of six people. When he was brought before the bench, the judge asked: "Are you ready to go to trial?"

"I am not ready, your honor," Gideon answered.

"Why aren't you ready?"

"I have no counsel."

"Why do you not have counsel? Did you not know that your case was set for trial today?"

Gideon then explained that he wanted the court to appoint a lawyer to help him.

The judge replied: "Mr. Gideon, I am sorry, but I can-not appoint counsel to represent you in this case. Under the laws of the State of Florida, the only time the court can appoint counsel to represent a defendant is when that person is charged with a capital offense. I am sorry, but I will have to deny your request. . . ."

Gideon then had to defend himself. The prosecutor (who was a lawyer, of course) had a key witness, a man named Henry Cook. Cook testified that he had seen Gideon come out of the pool hall in the dark early morning hours of the day of the break-in.

Gideon cross-examined Henry Cook and called eight witnesses himself. But he made little headway with the jury in his attempt to shake Cook's testimony. At the end of the trial, Gideon addressed the jury and strongly maintained that he was innocent. The jury did not agree and found him guilty. A short while later, Judge McCrary gave Gideon the maximum sentence possible, five years in the state penitentiary.

Clarence Gideon had dropped out of school after the eighth grade, but he was a clever and basically intelligent man. From his many encounters with the law, he had accumulated a fundamental understanding of legal issues, of the individual rights they involved, and of court procedures. It was this knowledge and the indignant feeling that he had been unjustly convicted in the pool hall burglary that prompted him to try to obtain his release from the Florida state prison.

First, Gideon filed a writ of *habeas corpus,* a claim that he was being held illegally in prison, with the supreme court of Florida. His writ was based on the argument that he had been denied certain rights because a lawyer was not provided for him at his trial. Florida's highest court, however, rejected that claim.

Gideon then wrote to the United States Supreme Court asking for an appeal of the state supreme court's ruling. It would seem unlikely that a poor, uneducated man, in prison after his fifth conviction, would have much chance convincing the Supreme Court to consider his case. But despite his amateur knowledge of the law and the fact that he had access to only a few law books in the prison library, Gideon had filed his request properly and according to the rules set forth by the Court. When the request was received in Washington, it went through the routine channels and finally reached the crucial point at which the court decides whether or not it will review the case.

In June 1962, the Supreme Court announced that it would consider Clarence Gideon's case. Gideon had applied for review *in forma pauperis,* that is, as a pauper. Because he was so poor, Gideon claimed, the Supreme Court would have to appoint a lawyer to present his case. The Supreme Court agreed and named Abe Fortas, a senior partner in a highly respected Washington law firm and one of the top lawyers in that city. Fortas himself was later to be appointed a justice of the Supreme Court, but in 1962 it was his duty to appear before the Court, and he set about the enormous task of preparing the case for Clarence Earl Gideon.

As he developed his case, Abe Fortas knew that he was not merely asking the Supreme Court to decide that state courts be required to provide lawyers in *all* cases where a defendant could not afford one. He was also asking the Court to overrule a decision that an earlier Supreme Court had made on the same subject. In essence, Fortas was asking the justices to admit that an error had been made before.

Fortas built his argument around the fact that it was actually the 14th Amendment to the Constitution that required courts to appoint a lawyer for poor defendants. That amendment provides that *no state* may "deprive any person of life, liberty, or property, without due process of law, nor deny to any person within its jurisdiction the equal protection of the laws. . . ." In effect, Fortas pointed out that a person could not get a fair trial without a lawyer and, without a fair trial, any conviction that might result would be without the "due process of law" as guaranteed by the 14th Amendment. In addition, there would not be "equal protection of the laws" for those who could not afford a lawyer and those who could.

Fortas also argued that the decision in the Betts case 20 years earlier was a mistake and should be corrected. He asked the Court to reconsider in light of his arguments. By ruling in favor of Gideon, he said, the Court would overturn that decision and thus correct its error.

The lawyers for the state of Florida argued that, first, Gideon was not entitled to a lawyer under the Florida laws and, second, there was no evidence whatsoever that Gideon had not received a fair trial, In any case, the state lawyers argued, the decision to appoint lawyers for the poor in criminal cases should be left up to the individual states.

The Supreme Court found the arguments of Abe Fortas very convincing and reversed the decision in Florida against Clarence Earl Gideon. By doing so, the Court insured that in the future no accused person would ever be tried without a lawyer simply because he or she did not have enough money to hire one.

Justice Hugo Black, who had been on the Court 20 years earlier and had disagreed with the decision then on the Betts case, now was assigned to write the majority opinion in the Gideon case. His opinion admitted directly that the Court had been wrong in its earlier judgment. And in 1962, there was no disagreement on the point from any of the other eight Supreme Court justices.

In Florida, Gideon happily received the news that he had won his case and that he would be granted a new trial. At the second trial on the pool hall charge, he had a lawyer who handled his case well. This time the jury found him not guilty.

In the years between the cases of Betts and Gideon, Justice Hugo Black had said, "There can be no equal justice where the kind of trial a man gets depends on the amount of money he has." It had taken a long time, but through the case of Clarence Earl Gideon the ideal expressed by Justice Black finally became a reality.

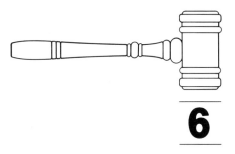

6

DONALD SEEGER

Religious Beliefs of a Conscientious Objector

The philosopher Friedrich Nietzsche once wrote, "Man shall be trained for war, woman for the recreation of the warrior. All else is folly." In more recent times the American general George S. Patton said, "Compared to war, all other forms of human endeavor shrink to insignificance. God, how I love it!"

It would be safe to say that most Americans do not agree with those views on the merits of war; killing, injuring, and destroying are not activities that most normal people like. Wars have existed as long as the human race itself, however, and millions of people have fought in them. But not all men have gone to war. Some have refused to fight, no matter what the cause, because they believed that all war is wrong. For them, participation in a war was forbidden by their religion, their beliefs, or their consciences. These are the people at the other end of the spectrum from Friedrich Nietzsche and General Patton.

The term used to identify a person who refuses to fight

A demonstration protesting American involvement in the Vietnam war

is "conscientious objector" — one who objects to war for reasons of conscience. At no time were American conscientious objectors more in evidence than during the nation's involvement in the Vietnam war of the 1960s and early 1970s. The reasons for this widespread resistance were many. Vietnam was a remote country that most Americans hardly knew existed before the war. The war itself had not been declared by Congress but had somehow grown until the United States had more than 500,000 men in the war zone. Not only was the Vietnam war an undeclared war, but it was also an unpopular one. It was a war that many Americans believed the United States should never have entered. Many people protested; a number even left the country and settled in nations like Canada and Sweden that honored their anti-war beliefs. Still other men of fighting age requested classification as conscientious objectors.

The history of conscientious objection in the United States goes back long before the war in Vietnam. It has been traced to the very beginnings of the nation. Among people who migrated to North America in the 1600s were many who belonged to religious groups that forbade their members to take up arms against other people. Perhaps the two most famous religious groups of this kind were the Quakers and the Mennonites. The followers of these religions did not join the colonial militia, nor would they fight against anyone, no matter what the cause.

It was not until the Civil War that a draft law was passed by Congress. This law empowered the United States to compel individuals to enter military service and fight in the war. The Confederate states also had a draft law, but laws in both North and South exempted those persons whose religious beliefs forbade them to fight.

After the Civil War, compulsory military service was no longer needed until the United States entered World War I in 1917. Then, a new draft law was passed. This law also exempted conscientious objectors, whom it identified as men belonging to a "well-recognized religious sect or organization [then] organized and existing and whose existing creed or principles [forbade] its members to participate in war in any form." This new law, however, required that conscientious objectors be drafted into the military to perform duties that did not require actual fighting. For example, they could be drafted into the medical corps or the supply corps.

A similar law went into effect at the beginning of World War II, and it added one other reason for exemption from fighting. A person could be classified as a conscientious objector if his opposition to war was based on "religious training and belief." What that meant was that the person did not have to belong to an organized religion or religious sect to be exempt from the draft as a conscientious objector. The objector could base his refusal to fight simply on "religious beliefs." Shortly after World War II, the law was again changed slightly so that the grounds for exemption were to be based not simply on "religious beliefs" but on beliefs that involved a relation to a "supreme being." The "supreme being" was described as the being commonly accepted as God by Protestants, Catholics, Jews, and other members of organized religions.

This was the existing law in 1957 when a young man named Donald Seeger asked to be classified as a conscientious objector. At the time, he was a student and was, therefore, exempt from the draft under a classification known as 2-S. Seeger, however, wanted to be excused from service permanently because of his beliefs. No action was taken on his case then, but in the following year, 1958, Donald Seeger was reclassified 1-A, which made him eligible for the draft. A board of the Selective Service System then took up Seeger's request for classification as a conscientious objector.

In a written statement, Seeger said he was conscientiously opposed to participation in any war by reason of his "religious beliefs." He chose, however, not to answer the question as to whether he believed in a supreme being. Seeger claimed that his "skepticism or disbelief in the existence of God" was not relevant. He explained that he did religiously hold a "belief in and devotion to goodness and virtue for their own sakes, and a religious faith in a purely ethical creed." In effect, Seeger said that he believed in everything a supreme being stood for, believed just as strongly as anyone who claimed to believe in God. But he himself did not necessarily believe in a supreme being in the same way most other people did.

The Selective Service System board accepted Seeger's arguments as sincere and honest. They agreed that his beliefs were of a "religious" nature and were held in good faith. Therefore, he qualified as a conscientious objector on the ground that his opposition to war was founded on "religious training and belief." But the board also said Seeger's "religious belief" was not based on a "relation to a supreme being." His request to be classified as conscientious objector was rejected for that last reason.

When the time came for Seeger to be inducted into the armed forces, he refused to report. He was arrested and brought to trial in the U.S. District Court for the Southern District of New York. At the trial, Seeger's arguments were the same as those he had made to the Selective Service System board. The federal government, which was prosecuting the case to uphold the draft regulation, argued the point again that Seeger did not qualify because he did not base his beliefs on "a relation to a supreme being." The court agreed with the government's lawyers, and Seeger was convicted of a violation of the selective service law.

Seeger appealed next to the United States Court of Appeals. This court agreed with Seeger and overruled the earlier conviction. The appeals court said that the requirement for belief in a supreme being could not be permitted if it made a distinction between people who, in their minds, formulated their own religious beliefs outside of an organized religion and people whose beliefs were determined by the organized groups to which they belonged. This, the court said, would be in violation of the 14th Amendment to the U.S. Constitution, which guarantees all persons "due process of law" and "equal protection of the laws."

The federal government appealed the ruling of the Court of Appeals to the United States Supreme Court. Seeger's case was not the only one brought before the Supreme Court to challenge the law in regard to conscientious objection. Another case from the same area of New York and one from California were to be heard along with Donald Seeger's case. The year was 1964, seven years since the day Seeger first requested classification as a conscientious objector. By this time, Americans were fighting in Vietnam.

Seeger's lawyers argued the case in much the same way as they had before the appeals court. Representing the federal government was United States Solicitor General Archibald Cox, a distinguished legal scholar. (Cox was to gain fame 10 years later as the special prosecutor in the Watergate investigation.) He presented the government's case: that Seeger did not qualify for exemption because he did not meet the full measure of the law's requirements in regard to "religious beliefs in a relation to a supreme being."

When the Court finally handed down its decision, it upheld the ruling of the appeals court and reversed Seeger's conviction as well as the convictions in the two

Thomas C. Clark

other cases. In the majority opinion, written by Justice Thomas C. Clark, it was noted that Seeger had never "disavowed" any belief in a supreme being; that is, he never said that he did not believe in some form of supreme being. In fact, Justice Clark added, Seeger had suggested that perhaps there was a "creative intelligence in the universe" that could be taken as a supreme being of sorts.

By means of the Supreme Court's decision, the law in regard to conscientious objectors was once again broadened. It now specified that a person's belief in or acceptance of a supreme being did not have to conform to the definitions set down by religious organizations or sects. The definition could be the result of religious beliefs developed entirely in the mind of an individual.

In 1967, heavyweight champion Muhammad Ali refused induction into the army because of his religious beliefs. Ali was convicted of draft evasion, but in 1974, the Supreme Court reversed the decision against him.

The law still does not extend to those who *deny* the existence of a supreme being, or to those who simply refuse to admit the existence of a supreme being. For this reason, the Court's decision in the Seeger case will probably not be the final word on the issue of conscientious objection to war. At the moment, there is no draft law in effect; therefore, no one is required to serve in the armed forces or to object on the basis of conscience. But if history repeats itself, as many believe it does, there will be another war of some kind, another draft law, other conscientious objectors, other challenges to the law, other trials, and other decisions on what truly constitutes "conscientious objection."

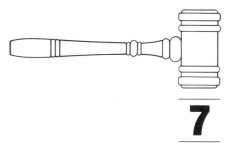

7

DANNY ESCOBEDO AND ERNESTO MIRANDA
Confessions and Rights Before Trial

The scene might be any city in the United States. A police officer arrests a suspected lawbreaker. Then, before the suspect can speak, the officer recites some words that sound as if they were memorized: "I must tell you first you have the right to remain silent. If you choose not to remain silent, anything you say or write can and will be used as evidence against you in court. You have the right to consult a lawyer before any questioning, and you have the right to have the lawyer present with you during any questioning. You not only have the right to consult with a lawyer before any questioning, but if you lack the financial ability to retain a lawyer, a lawyer will be appointed to represent you before any questioning, and to be present with you during any questioning."

As this scene suggests, an officer of the law cannot simply arrest a person suspected of a crime and rush him or her down to the jailhouse. There are definite procedures that must be followed in making an arrest. The interrogation, or questioning, of the suspect also has to follow certain rules and limitations. If the suspect confesses to the crime, that confession may be presented as evidence in court only if it has been obtained without the use of force, trickery, or other unfair methods. What is more, a confession can be used as legal evidence only if all the individual's rights have been explained and are *understood* by the person.

There was a time, however, not so long ago, when such rights were not spelled out. Beating a confession out of someone has always been against the law in the United States, but laws have been overlooked from time to time. For example, in a Chicago police station in 1936, a 19-year-old black youth, Earl Pugh, was told that he was being charged with murder, even though he had been arrested on suspicion of robbery in a case that had no connection with the murder. He was advised by the police to confess to the murder, but he refused. For six days Earl Pugh insisted firmly that he was innocent in the murder case. For those six days, he was given only enough food and water to stay alive. He was questioned almost continually and was beaten severely during that time. Finally, with one arm broken and his body covered with bruises, Pugh agreed to sign the confession.

A jury found Pugh guilty on the strength of only one piece of evidence, his confession. Pugh was sentenced to prison for life. He remained in jail for 17 years until a lawyer became interested in the case and began to check the records. The lawyer discovered that when Pugh had been tried, the prosecution actually had testimony from two eyewitnesses who said the killer had been a *white* man. The prosecuting attorney had chosen not to report that information either to the court or to Pugh's lawyer.

Ten years later, in Chicago again, a young girl, Suzanne Degnan, was kidnapped and murdered. The police suspected a janitor in the neighborhood, brought him in for questioning, and finally got a confession from him. In the process of obtaining that confession, however, officers had beaten the janitor so badly that he was crippled for life. Despite his confession, the janitor was never brought to trial because the real killer was finally caught.

Chicago was not the only American city whose police obtained confessions by using such brutal methods. As late as 1961, a federal government commission on civil rights reported that "the use of physical brutality and violence is not, unfortunately, relegated to the past or to any part of the country."

Besides physical beating, other methods have been used to squeeze confessions out of people. Although less painful, these methods are equally unfair to the person accused. Refusing to let a suspect call a lawyer or any other person until the suspect has signed a confession is a tactic that has been used in many cities, large and small, even though it is illegal. Another method is to frighten suspects by threatening physical beatings or some other consequence so serious that they confess only to save themselves.

Such methods were illegal before the 1960s, just as they are now. But there were other methods that were within the law and were outlined in careful detail in manuals distributed to police departments. Earl Warren, when he was chief justice of the Supreme Court, described the methods and branded them as unfair when he wrote:

From these . . . interrogation techniques, the setting prescribed by the manuals and observed in practice becomes clear. In essence, it is this: To be alone with the suspect is essential to prevent distraction and to deprive him of any outside support. The aura of confidence in his guilt undermines his will to resist. He merely confirms the preconceived story the police seek to have him describe. Patience and persistence, at times relentless questioning, are employed. To obtain a confession, the interrogator must "patiently maneuver himself or his quarry into a position from which the desired object may be obtained." When normal procedures fail to produce the needed result, the police may resort to deceptive strategems such as giving false legal advice. It is important to keep the subject off balance, for example, by trading on his insecurity about himself or his surroundings. The police then persuade, trick, or cajole him out of exercising his constitutional rights.

In 1964 and 1966, two important cases came before the United States Supreme Court that forced police departments throughout the country to change the ways in which they questioned suspects and obtained confessions.

The important cases involved two young men, Danny Escobedo and Ernesto Miranda. They were arrested in completely separate cases, but they did have one thing in common: the way each was treated after being arrested.

Danny Escobedo was 22 years old and living in Chicago in 1960. In the early hours of January 20, he was arrested and taken to the police station for questioning about the murder of his brother-in-law, which had taken place a few hours earlier. He made no statement to police, and after about 14 hours his lawyer obtained a release and Escobedo went home.

Ten days later, however, police officers arrived at his house again and this time arrested both Escobedo and his sister, the murder victim's wife. They handcuffed Escobedo and led him out to a waiting police car. On the way to the station, one of the police officers told Escobedo that his friend Benedict DiGerlando had said that Escobedo had fired the shots that killed the victim.

"We've got a pretty tight case against you," the policeman added. "For your own good you might as well admit the crime."

"I'm sorry, but I'd like to have advice from my lawyer," Escobedo answered.

After learning of the arrest, Escobedo's lawyer went directly to the police station. There he was told by a police sergeant that his client had been taken to the homicide bureau for questioning.

"I asked Sergeant Pidgeon for permission to speak to my client," the lawyer testified later, "and he [the sergeant] told me I could not see him." Escobedo's lawyer then went directly to the homicide bureau and asked again to speak with his client. Again permission was refused. The lawyer waited for another hour or two, occasionally talking to some of the detectives and continuing to ask to speak with Escobedo. At one point, the lawyer caught a glimpse of his client through an open door and waved. Escobedo waved back and then the door was closed quickly. Finally the lawyer quoted to the police officer in charge a section of the criminal code that gives a lawyer the right to see his client. Then he left to file an official complaint with the Chicago police commissioner.

While all this was going on, Escobedo was being questioned but he would not make any statement. Finally, the police brought DiGerlando into the room, and the two young men met face to face.

"I didn't shoot Manuel, you did it," Escobedo shouted.

Unfortunately for Escobedo, that was an admission that he knew about the crime. Escobedo realized he had made a bad mistake. After a few more hours of questioning, Escobedo said that he had paid DiGerlando $500 to shoot the victim. An assistant state's attorney was brought in, and he carefully wrote down Escobedo's statement, making sure that everything was in a form that would be admissible in court.

At his trial, Danny Escobedo said the confession was untrue and that he had been tricked into making it. Escobedo claimed that the police told him that if he would sign the statement, he would be allowed to go home and would not be prosecuted. The police denied making such an offer. Escobedo's lawyer tried to have the confession thrown out of court, but the judge decided against him, and the confession was allowed as evidence. Escobedo was convicted and sentenced to life imprisonment.

His lawyer appealed the case, but the Illinois Supreme Court upheld the original verdict. An appeal was then made to the United States Supreme Court on the grounds that Escobedo had wrongly been denied the right to consult with his lawyer, and that he had not been informed of his right to remain silent.

More than four years after the crime, the Supreme Court passed down its decision. "We granted . . . to consider whether the petitioner's [Escobedo's] statement

Arthur Goldberg

was constitutionally admissable at his trial. We conclude for the reasons stated below that it was not and accordingly we reverse the judgment of conviction."

Justice Arthur Goldberg wrote the majority opinion and explained the reasons for reversing the conviction of Escobedo. Justice Goldberg said Escobedo's lawyer should have been allowed to talk with him at the police station before he was questioned. In effect, Escobedo had been denied the right to counsel guaranteed by the 6th Amendment of the United States Constitution, a right that was guaranteed in state as well as federal proceedings by the 14th Amendment. The issues of the suspect's right to remain silent and the requirement that the suspect be told that anything he or she did say could be used as evidence in court was not ruled upon at the

Danny Escobedo *(left),* accompanied by his attorney, Barry Kroll, leaves the Cook Country Jail in Chicago after the Supreme Court reversed his conviction in August 1964.

time. That was to come two years later, in 1966, after the Supreme Court heard the case of Ernesto Miranda.

About a year before the Escobedo decision was reached in the Supreme Court, Ernesto Miranda was arrested at his home in Phoenix, Arizona, on suspicion of the kidnapping and rape of an 18-year-old girl. At the police station, the girl who had made the complaint said that Miranda was indeed the person who had kidnapped and raped her. Miranda was then taken to a room for questioning. He was not told that he was entitled to have a lawyer present during the questioning, nor was he told clearly that he had the right to remain silent and that anything he did say could be used against him in court.

Miranda realized he was in serious trouble because he had been identified by the victim. Possibly for this reason, he confessed quickly. He explained his version of the crime to the police officers questioning him. A written statement was then drawn up beginning with a paragraph that stated that the confession was a voluntary one, made without threats or promises of immunity from prosecution and made with "full knowledge of my legal rights, understanding any statement I make may be used against me." Miranda signed the confession and was held for trial.

At the trial, Miranda's lawyer objected to allowing that confession to be introduced as evidence, but he was overruled. The jury found Miranda guilty of both kidnapping and rape, and he was given terms of 20 to 30 years imprisonment on each charge. The sentences were to run concurrently (at the same time) rather than one sentence after the other.

The case was then appealed to the Arizona Supreme Court on the grounds that Miranda had not been allowed to talk with a lawyer before being questioned and that during the questioning he had not been truly aware of the consequences of what he said to the police. Miranda claimed he did not realize that what he told the police could be used against him at the trial. Arizona's supreme court ruled against Miranda, noting that in the signed statement Miranda did admit he "understood" that the statement could be used against him. Furthermore, the court said, Miranda had not specifically requested a lawyer and, therefore, the police were not required to provide counsel for him.

Miranda's case reached the United States Supreme Court in 1966. In a majority opinion, Chief Justice Earl Warren referred to the Court's decision in the case of Danny Escobedo and pointed out its importance in providing protection for individuals against overzealous police practices. Chief Justice Warren wrote: "The constitutional issue we decide . . . is the admissibility of statements obtained from a defendant questioned while in custody and deprived of his freedom of action."

The case that Chief Justice Warren was writing about was certainly a difficult one. On one hand, there was the important question of the rights of a person under the protection of the Constitution. On the other hand, there was the equally important issue of interfering with the work of the police and preventing them from arresting criminals and bringing them to trial. Members of the Supreme Court were deeply divided on how the Court should rule.

The smallest possible majority of five justices to four made the historic ruling: ". . . it is clear that Miranda was not in any way apprised of his right to consult with an

Earl Warren

attorney and to have one present during the interrogation, nor was his right not to be compelled to incriminate himself effectively protected in any other manner. Without these warnings the statements were inadmissible. The mere fact that he signed a statement which contained a typed-in clause stating that he had 'full knowledge' of his 'legal rights' does not approach the knowing and intelligent waiver required to relinquish constitutional rights."

With those words, the guilty verdict against Ernesto Miranda was reversed. Police departments throughout the country from that day forward would have to be much more careful about the constitutional rights of individuals. The Miranda case, like the earlier Escobedo case, firmly established those rights as guaranteed by the Constitution.

As a result of the Supreme Court's decisions, the names of Danny Escobedo and Ernesto Miranda became famous, and both men were set free. The rulings of the Supreme Court have endured, but the freedom of the two men did not last. In 1968, Escobedo was convicted of selling narcotics and was sentenced to 22 years in an Illinois prison. Miranda was convicted of armed robbery in 1967, and was sentenced to 20-25 years in the Arizona state prison. After being paroled he was arrested again in 1974 for possession of a hand gun. This final charge was later dropped. In the spring of 1976, almost 10 years after the Supreme Court decision that made his name important in legal history, Ernesto Miranda was stabbed to death in a bar fight.

Ernesto Miranda

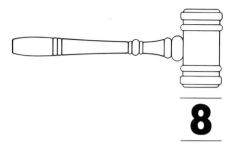

GERALD GAULT
The Rights of Juveniles

Gerald Gault was a 15-year-old boy who decided one day to make an obscene telephone call. He was sentenced to six years in a state reform school for doing it. Eventually, the case of Gerald Gault was brought before the United States Supreme Court, with results that would have a significant influence on the legal rights of young people in the American court system.

Special courts for young offenders had been established long before Gerald Gault was born in 1949. Their purpose was to treat juveniles separately and to keep them out of the system of criminal justice for adults. Before the establishment of such courts, young people in the United States had received the same kind of justice as that allotted to adults. It was not uncommon for children as young as seven to be given long prison terms and even death sentences. There is, in fact, a record from the nation's early history of an eight-year-old child who was hanged for the crime of setting a fire.

As time went on, however, adults began to think that perhaps they were being too harsh with young people who broke certain rules or committed crimes. Judges, lawyers, and thoughtful people everywhere began to consider the idea of treating young lawbreakers differently than adults. Finally, in 1899, the first juvenile court was established in Chicago, Illinois. Soon after, similar juvenile courts were set up in all the states.

The juvenile courts are quite different from the criminal courts where adults are put on trial. The same kinds of cases may be heard in both courts — everything from littering to murder — but they are handled in very different ways. The idea behind the juvenile court is that it exists to act as a "protective parent" instead of a prosecutor. Its goal is to help and protect young offenders rather than to punish them for crimes that they may not really understand. Since the court acts as a substitute parent, it is responsible not only for delinquent youths but also for dependent and neglected youngsters.

A juvenile case is not a criminal proceeding, no matter what the offense. In an adult criminal case, there is a formal trial with defined court rules. Any particular crime will fall into a specific category, and there is a set range of punishments for each kind of crime. In the juvenile court, each case is treated by itself and is considered only in terms of the particular person and circumstances involved. The findings of the court are not limited by a specific range of punishments as are adult trials. Instead, the juvenile court's responsibility is to determine in each individual case what care or supervision is necessary or best to help young people overcome habits of delinquency. The idea of a juvenile court is to be just in a legal sense and also to be helpful to the young. But it has not always worked out that way, as Gerald Gault unhappily found out.

In 1964, when Gerald Gault was 15, his family lived in Gila County, Arizona, a sprawling area of desert, mountains, canyons, and small towns east of Phoenix, Arizona's biggest city. One hot, dusty morning in June of that year, Gerald met with a friend, Ronnie Lewis, to decide what to do that day. Their choice was unfortunate.

One of the boys picked up the telephone and dialed the number of Mrs. Ora Cook. When she answered the phone, the boys made some obscene remarks and suggestions. Mrs. Cook listened and then slammed down the phone. One of the voices was quite familiar, she thought. It sounded very much like a neighborhood teenager — Gerald Gault. So she picked up her phone again and called the Gila County sheriff to tell him about her suspicions. Later that morning, the sheriff arrested the two boys and took them to a juvenile detention home.

Gerald's father was out of town on business at the time, and his mother didn't get home from work until about six o'clock that evening. When Gerald did not show up for dinner, Mrs. Gault sent his older brother to look for him. He went to Ronnie Lewis' house, where he was told that Gerald was being held at the juvenile home.

Gerald's brother and his mother went to the home to find out what had happened. They met with a probation officer named Flagg, who told them about the phone call. He said that Gerald would have to be held at the juvenile home until a hearing the next day in juvenile court.

Gerald, it seems, had an additional problem: he was already on probation. Two years earlier, he and another boy had been involved in a petty theft. Because Gerald had apparently violated his probation, the juvenile officer had sufficient reason to hold him in custody.

After the Gaults left, the probation officer wrote a petition and filed it with the juvenile court. It stated that Gerald Gault was a delinquent minor on probation from the court and asked for a hearing on what should be done about his care and custody. The petition did not mention why Gerald had been arrested that morning. No copy of the document was given to the Gaults.

The next day, Gerald, his mother, and his brother appeared in juvenile court before Judge McGhee. Flagg and another juvenile officer also were present. The judge himself questioned Gerald, and after a while the youth admitted that he had dialed the telephone of Mrs. Ora Cook.

Mrs. Gault was worried. She could see that Gerald's act violated the conditions of his probation, and she realized that her son was definitely in trouble. Yet she hoped the judge would be lenient because the telephone call, although offensive to Mrs. Cook, was hardly a serious crime. As the hearing was coming to a close, Mrs. Gault asked the judge if he was planning to send Gerald to the state industrial school.

"No . . . I'll think it over," was his answer.

The judge then ended the session, told the Gaults that they would be notified when the next hearing was to take place, and sent Gerald back to the juvenile home. A few days later Gerald was allowed to go to his own home for the weekend. On the same day, his mother received notice that the next hearing would be held the following Monday morning.

At that hearing, Gerald and both his parents appeared before Judge McGhee. The two juvenile officers were present again. Another report had been filed with the court by Officer Flagg, this time charging Gerald with having made lewd and obscene remarks in the presence of a woman. No copy of this report was given to the Gaults, and they didn't even know it had been made.

Mrs. Gault requested that Mrs. Cook, the person who had made the complaint, be called to testify. Judge McGhee said that testimony from Mrs. Cook would not be necessary. Then he began the hearing. The judge said he remembered that Gerald had admitted, at the first hearing, to making some of the obscene remarks. The Gaults denied this. They said that Gerald had only confessed to having dialed the telephone. Officer Flagg said he couldn't remember, but thought that the Gaults were right. There was no way to find out whose memory was correct, because, following usual juvenile court practice, no records of the previous hearing had been kept.

After more questioning and some additional discussion of what went on at the first hearing, Judge McGhee reached a decision. He ruled Gerald to be delinquent and ordered him confined to the state reform school, until he reached 21 years of age. If Gerald Gault had been an adult found guilty of the same charge, his sentence might have been a fine of $5 to $50 or a prison term of not more than two months. As a youth, however, he was sentenced to the reform school for a period of six years.

The Gaults felt that this action was neither just nor merciful, but there was little they could do about it. The state law did not provide for appealing juvenile cases to a higher court. Therefore, both the findings of delinquency and the decision to confine Gerald for six years could not be challenged.

Gerald Gault went off to the Arizona state reformatory. While he was there, however, his parents filed a writ of *habeas corpus,* that is, a petition for a hearing on the legality of confinement. In effect, the writ claimed that Gerald was being held in the reformatory illegally. This was the only way the Gaults could use the law to seek a review of Gerald's case. The writ was referred to a superior court for hearing, but the court apparently felt that Gerald's confinement was legal and dismissed the writ.

The Gaults then appealed this ruling to the state supreme court. Meanwhile, Gerald remained in the reformatory. The Gaults and their lawyer argued for the writ of *habeas corpus* on the grounds that Gerald had been denied "due process of law." They were not asking the court to overrule the juvenile judge's decision about the phone call, but they were claiming that their son had been denied basic and constitutional rights during the juvenile court proceedings. Therefore, the boy was confined illegally and should be released, the Gaults said.

The state supreme court did not share their views, and upheld dismissal of the Gaults' writ of *habeas corpus* action. This ruling was then appealed to the United States Supreme Court. The Court agreed to review the issues of the case; it was only the second time in the history of the United States that the Supreme Court had reviewed a juvenile proceeding.

The Gaults' lawyer based his case on six points in which he claimed Gerald had been denied due process of law. Gerald, he said,

had not been granted the right to counsel;
had not been informed of his right to remain silent
or told that what he said could be used against him;

These nine justices sat on the Supreme Court in 1967, when the Gault case was reviewed: *(seated, left to right),* Tom C. Clark, Hugo L. Black, Chief Justice Earl Warren, William O. Douglas, and John M. Harlan; *(standing, left to right)* Byron R. White, William J. Brennan, Jr., Potter Stewart, and Abe Fortas.

had not been given the right to confront and cross-examine the witness against him;

had been denied the right of formal notice of the hearings, the charges, and the possible consequences of his act;

had not had the right to appeal his case to a higher court; and

had been denied the right to a record of the proceedings against him.

These were rights and protections guaranteed by the Constitution. These rights should have been guaranteed to Gerald Gault, his lawyer claimed, even though Gerald was a minor and his case was in a juvenile court. The lawyer for the state of Arizona disagreed. He argued that because a juvenile court hearing was not a criminal matter, certain rights were not guaranteed. The juvenile court was not prosecuting and punishing the defendant in the way courts would handle an adult case. It was acting as a *protective parent,* prescribing specific treatment for the youth based solely on the circumstances of his individual case.

As to specific rights claimed by Gerald Gault, the state's lawyer attacked them one by one:

The right to counsel. In a juvenile case, parents can employ a lawyer if they desire, but the court was not required to provide a lawyer in the Gault case because it was not a criminal proceeding.

The right to remain silent. Because Gerald's trial was not a criminal trial, this right was not guaranteed. In fact, if the right were provided, the juvenile court judge would be hampered in determining the best "treatment" for the offender.

The right to confront witnesses. Gerald did not deny the charges against him; he even admitted to some of them. Therefore, there was no reason to cross-examine the woman who made the complaint.

The right of formal notice. Officer Flagg's informal notice was sufficient because this was not a criminal trial.

The right of appeal. State law prohibited the appeal of any juvenile case. That was simply the law in existence.

The right to records of the hearings. Because there was no right of appeal, there was no reason to keep records of the hearings.

The lawyer for the state of Arizona also argued that to grant all these rights would destroy the juvenile court system as it was then set up. For a juvenile court to function properly as a protective parent, the proceedings

Abe Fortas

have to be flexible and informal. Otherwise, the proceedings would be placed back on the level of an adult criminal trial.

The Supreme Court listened to both arguments. Then, on May 15, 1967, almost three years after Gerald Gault's ill-fated telephone call, it handed down its decision. The Court ruled in favor of Gerald Gault on four of the six points. It held that he had indeed been denied the "due process of law" as guaranteed in the 14th Amendment to the Constitution.

Justice Abe Fortas wrote the Court's opinion. He said that juvenile hearings are, in effect, criminal proceedings. Young people are taken from the custody of their parents and confined to state institutions. Because of these serious consequences, they should be guaranteed the protection of the Constitution.

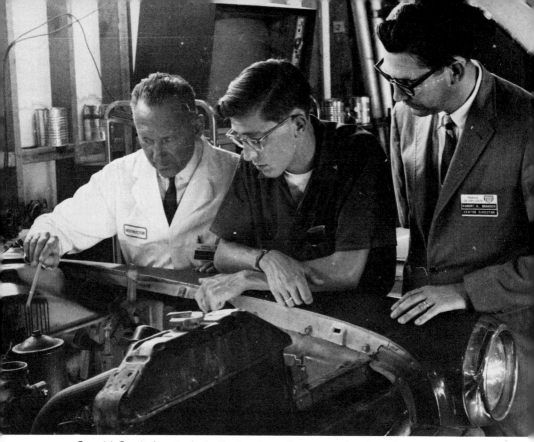

Gerald Gault *(center)* studied automotive operation in a Job Corps center after his release from the reformatory in 1967.

Gerald Gault had finally won his case and had been released from the reformatory. As a result of his experience with the legal system, many of the procedures in a juvenile hearing would be changed. The basic idea of the juvenile court system was not destroyed, as the lawyers of the state of Arizona feared. The juvenile court would still act as a protective parent and not as a prosecutor and punisher of criminals. The changes brought about by the case of Gerald Gault, however, clearly provided certain basic rights and protections that did not exist before. These changes served to strengthen the system, thereby making it more just.

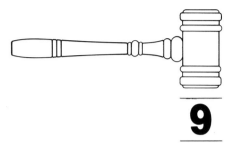

9

RALPH BERGER
Wiretapping and the Right to Privacy

Eavesdropping is a practice that is probably as old as civilization itself. In ancient times, eavesdroppers had to use "ear-to-the-door, eye-to-the-keyhole" methods in order to spy on their neighbors. Later, binoculars and earhorns helped the snoopers in their work. Then the age of electronics added an entirely new dimension to the art of prying into private affairs.

The telephone was invented in 1876 by Alexander Graham Bell, and with it was born a new form of eavesdropping known as "wiretapping." Wiretapping became such a nuisance that it was outlawed in several states as early as 1895. But other forms of electronic eavesdropping grew in direct proportion to our knowledge of instruments to catch and reproduce sounds. Now there are electronic devices smaller than a postage stamp that can be hidden in a room and can pick up whispers and broadcast them to a receiver a half mile away. The common term for this type of eavesdropping is "bugging."

Under the leadership of J. Edgar
Hoover, the FBI made extensive use
of bugging to gather information.

Bugging has become very widespread in modern society. Police and government law enforcement agencies have routinely used "bugs." The FBI has admitted that it used bugging to get information about people as different as a Mafia hoodlum and Martin Luther King, and that it even wiretapped the telephone in Joe Namath's bar. Bugs are obviously employed by spies in many kinds of intelligence-gathering activities. Businesses, private detectives, and even private citizens have been known to use bugging devices for their own varied reasons. And no one will ever forget the politically motivated bugging of the Democratic National Headquarters at Watergate in 1972, or the fact that former President Richard Nixon had bugged himself by recording conversations that took place in his private office.

As the art of eavesdropping has improved and its use become more widespread, the laws against improper use of snooping devices have increased as well. By 1967, wiretapping was generally prohibited in all but a very few states, but practically every state permitted it in the interest of law enforcement. Most state laws required that such official use of wiretapping be authorized and ordered by a court. Bugging, however, was permitted both by authorized officials and by private citizens in all but seven states.

New York was one of the states that had a law authorizing judges to issue orders for eavesdropping by the police. Ralph Berger, a public relations man from Chicago, found that out, much to his discomfort.

It all began in 1966 in New York City among people Ralph Berger did not even know. One day Ralph Pansini, the owner of a New York bar and grill, was visited by agents of the New York state liquor authority. The agents seized Pansini's books and records and took them to their offices. Pansini was enraged and went to the district attorney's office. He claimed that he was being harrassed by the agents because he had refused to pay a bribe when applying for his liquor license. Besides complaining to the district attorney, Pansini was willing to prove what he said.

The district attorney was interested in Pansini's story. He sent Pansini back to the state liquor authority's office, this time with a tiny recording device hidden on his body. When Pansini asked about settling the matter and getting

Harry Neyer

back his business records, an employee of the liquor authority told him the "price" for a license was $10,000. Pansini was told to contact an attorney named Harry Neyer. All of the incriminating conversation was recorded by the tiny instrument that Pansini was carrying.

With this evidence as a start, the district attorney went to the New York Supreme Court and asked for a court order to bug Harry Neyer's law office for more information. The order was granted to permit electronic eavesdropping for 60 days.

At the end of the two-month period, the district attorney had a few leads based on information gained from the bugging. Because of this, another request was put to the state supreme court for another bugging, this one to be placed in the office of another person suspected of being involved with the bribes. It too, was approved.

At this point, Ralph Berger entered the scene. By means of this second bug, the district attorney learned of a conspiracy to bribe public officials in order to obtain liquor licenses for two clubs, the Playboy Club and the Tenement Club. Ralph Berger turned out to be the "go-between" through whom the clubs would deal with the person being bribed at the state liquor authority.

Berger was arrested in connection with the bribery conspiracy and brought to trial. In court, portions of the recordings from the bugging were introduced as evidence by the prosecution. Ralph Berger's lawyers objected strongly, but they were overruled. The jury found Berger guilty on two counts of conspiracy to bribe the chairman of the New York Liquor Authority.

After the trial, Berger's lawyer claimed that not only was the conviction unfair but also the arrest and the very fact of Berger's being brought to trial. They pointed out that the district attorney "had no information upon which to proceed to present a case to the Grand Jury, or on the basis of which to prosecute" Berger, except for the evidence gained from eavesdropping. They then appealed the case, claiming the evidence was gotten illegally.

Berger's appeal failed on the state level and also in the federal court of appeals. So he took his case to the United States Supreme Court. The grounds for Berger's appeal were that the New York statute under which he was convicted was unconstitutional. This statute authorized judges to issue orders for eavesdropping when requested by certain law enforcement officials and when there were reasonable grounds to believe that evidence of a crime might be uncovered by such eavesdropping. Berger's lawyers claimed that the state statute violated the rights of an individual guaranteed by the 4th, 5th, 9th, and 14th amendments to the United States Constitution. The New York statute, they said, unconstitutionally invaded and violated the privacy of an individual, authorized "general searches" for "mere evidence," and violated an individual's privilege against self-incrimination.

Lawyers for the state of New York argued, of course, that the statute was legal and constitutional. They said that the law had been followed strictly in connection with Berger's arrest, trial, and conviction. Therefore, the conviction should stand.

The Supreme Court listened to both arguments and then took up consideration of earlier Court rulings on the subjects of wiretapping and bugging. A well-known case of wiretapping was *Olmstead* v. *United States,* in which evidence against a bootlegger named Olmstead was gathered by tapping his telephone. That particular wiretap, however, was not attached directly to Olmstead's telephone, but was connected to the telephone wire *outside* his house. Because it was outside, the state had argued, it was not an unlawful invasion, or search, of "persons, houses, papers, and effects," which are protected by the 4th Amendment. The Supreme Court in 1928 did not see it that way, however, and overruled the conviction.

As far as bugging went, the Court considered several past cases but noted particularly *Silverman* v. *United*

States. In that case, the officials who were bugging Silverman had not actually entered his apartment but instead had driven a 12-inch nail equipped with a tiny microphone through a wall until it entered a heating duct that ran throughout Silverman's apartment. The Court judged that it was still an unlawful trespass and ruled in favor of Silverman.

The Berger case, as it was presented to the Supreme Court in 1967, was a broader and much more difficult case than those that the Court had heard in the past. It had also aroused a great deal of controversy. On one side were those who spoke strongly for the individual right to privacy and the avoidance of police-state tactics. On the other side were those who argued with equal strength and vigor for effective law enforcement and the use of scientific and engineering advances that would help in both the prevention of crimes and the solution of crimes. Both sides presented some very good legal points.

The Supreme Court announced its decision in the Berger case on June 12, 1967. It was not a unanimous decision — the justices were divided six to three — but the majority ruled in favor of Berger and reversed the lower court's decision. The majority opinion was written by Justice Thomas C. Clark. In it, he noted that the case was only being considered in terms of the 4th and 14th amendments. The issue would be whether bugging is an invasion of privacy, a violation of the "right of the people to be secure in their persons, houses, papers, and effects, against unreasonable searches and seizures . . ." The other grounds for appeal presented by Berger's lawyers would not be considered.

Justice Clark wrote that the New York statute was too

broad in its coverage and, indeed, allowed intrusion on the privacy of the defendant. "In short, the statute's blanket grant of permission to eavesdrop is without adequate judicial supervision or protective procedures." Berger's rights under the 4th and 14th amendments had been violated.

The Berger case was the most important one in regard to electronic eavesdropping to have been considered by the Supreme Court. It was also the case in which the Court made its broadest ruling. Since the Berger ruling, Congress has moved firmly in the direction of controlling the use of electronic eavesdropping with appropriate laws. It is still an issue, however, and will doubtless continue to be one for quite some time. Even if electronic eavesdropping is restricted solely to cases involving "grave national security," decisions as to who may be bugged must be made by officials authorized to define the risks to national security. Just a few years ago, those "risks" apparently included Martin Luther King, Joe Namath, and the Democratic National Committee.

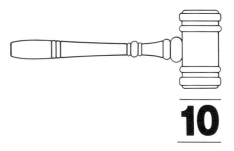

10

ALLAN BAKKE
Affirmative Action

Allan Bakke was grim when he read the letter from the university early in 1973. The brief message informed him that his application to the medical school at the University of California at Davis had been rejected. It wasn't the rejection itself that disturbed Bakke so much, for 10 other medical schools had already turned him down. He was upset about what he felt had been the reason for his rejection — the color of his skin. Bakke believed that he had been refused admittance to the Davis medical school because he was white.

The 100 openings for freshman medical students at Davis were filled according to an "affirmative action" admissions policy. Sixteen of those openings were reserved for students who were members of minority groups: Black, Asian, or Hispanic. Applicants with minority group backgrounds were permitted to compete for all 100 vacancies, but white students, no matter how good their academic qualifications, could compete for only 84 slots — the ones

103

not assigned to minority students. The result was that among the students admitted in 1973 were several minority group members with lower academic test scores than Allan Bakke, whose score was in the top 10 percent of those who had taken the medical school admission tests.

After he was turned down, Bakke wrote a letter to the University of California criticizing its admissions policies. He applied again for admission to Davis in the summer of 1973, and he was rejected again. This time, there was some evidence that his complaints about the treatment he had received previously were taken into account in rejecting him once more. There seemed to be only one way for Bakke to gain admission to medical school. That was to start a lawsuit and try to force Davis to accept him.

In June 1974, Bakke's lawyer filed suit on his behalf in the Superior Court of Yolo County, California. The suit charged that the university's admissions policy was a violation of Bakke's rights under the California Constitution, under Title VI of the 1964 Civil Rights Act, and under the 14th Amendment to the United States Constitution, which provides that no state shall deny any person the equal protection of the law.

In many ways Allan Paul Bakke seemed an unlikely person to place himself willingly in a position of public attention and controversy. A very quiet and private man, Bakke took elaborate steps to shield himself, his wife, and their two children from any personal publicity during the time his case was being tried. He refused all requests for interviews and for photographs. Pictures that were taken of Bakke frequently showed him shielding his face from the camera with books or newspapers. But Allan

Allan Bakke

Bakke's withdrawn, reserved manner concealed a fierce determination to right the great injustice that he felt had been done him.

Born in Minneapolis, Minnesota, of Norwegian ancestry, Bakke was the son of a mailman and a school teacher. He had become interested in medicine relatively late in life. Bakke had trained as an engineer and had served four years in the Marines, including seven months in Vietnam. He was 32 years old at the time his first application to Davis was rejected.

The first judicial decision in the Bakke case came shortly after a suit was filed in June. In November 1974, a Yolo County Superior Court judge, F. Leslie Manker, ruled that the Davis admissions program had discriminated against Bakke because of his race and, therefore, was invalid. The judge declined Bakke's request that he be admitted to Davis, however. His decision was limited to an order that the university decide Bakke's application without taking his race into consideration. Since neither Bakke nor the University of California had received the relief they sought, both parties appealed the court's order. Though the appeal would normally have gone from the trial court to an intermediate level appellate court, the importance of the case caused the California Supreme Court to decide to hear it directly on appeal.

The California Supreme Court is regarded as one of the most able in the state court system, and its decisions are frequently cited by other courts and by legal scholars. Therefore, its decision in the Bakke case would be an important one. In September 1976, the court decided unanimously that the Davis affirmative action program was unconstitutional because it deprived whites of the equal protection of the law. Bakke was ordered to be admitted to the Davis medical school in the fall.

Many civil rights leaders hoped the Bakke case would end there. They were afraid that if an appeal were taken to the United States Supreme Court, all affirmative action programs would be declared unconstitutional. If that happened, many of the benefits that had been so painfully secured by the civil rights movement would be lost. Nonetheless, the University of California decided to appeal the California Supreme Court ruling. In February 1977 the United States Supreme Court agreed to hear the case. The stage was now set for a decision by the nation's supreme judicial authority on what many felt would be the most important civil rights case since the integration decision in *Brown* v. *Board of Education* nearly a quarter of a century earlier.

Unlike people of many other nations, Americans have often turned to their courts rather than their elected leaders in establishing national policy on the great social issues of the day. Certainly this has been true in the area of civil rights. In the 19th century, the Supreme Court's decision in the Dred Scott case upheld white Southern control over runaway slaves, even when they escaped to free states. The Dred Scott case caused many abolitionists to feel that there were no legal means of ending slavery and thus hastened the start of the Civil War. *Plessy* v. *Ferguson* (1896) established the "separate but equal" doctrine and served as a means of keeping blacks in a position of inferiority to whites for nearly a hundred years. Then, in 1954, the decision of the Supreme Court in *Brown* v. *Board of Education* reversed *Plessy* v. *Ferguson.*

After the Brown case, enormous changes took place in the legal status of minority group members. Massive efforts were also made to raise minority economic and educational levels both by governmental and private programs. Among the most controversial of these programs was affirmative action, which lay at the heart of the Bakke controversy. Affirmative action programs were designed to provide special preference in education and employment opportunities for primarily blacks, who had previously been denied these opportunities because of discrimination. This special preference was given in order to insure that a certain number of jobs and school slots would be filled by minority group members.

The use of affirmative action raised the question of just how far a society could or should go in making up for the effects of past discrimination. As Americans faced this question, many different answers emerged. Some people felt that race should not be taken into account in any decision involving competition for a job or educational opportunity. They believed that these matters should be decided wholly on merit. According to this view, affirmative action was a device for establishing fixed quotas for members of racial groups. It was actually a form of "reverse discrimination," by means of which whites would be treated in the same unjust way that minority group members had been treated in the past.

Those who supported affirmative action pointed to a need for some kind of program that gave special preference to minorities in order to overcome the effects of past discrimination. Because members of minority groups had been denied equal opportunities in the past, they were now *under-represented* in the fields of employment and education. In other words, fewer minority group members had good jobs and were well educated than would be expected from the number of minorities in the population as a whole. In order to make up for this lack, minorities should be entitled to over-representation in employment and education for as long as it was necessary for them to catch up to the white majority population. This policy was justified not only as a compensation for past injustice but also as a means of improving the racial situation in the future. If more representatives of minority groups achieved positions of importance in employment and education, they would provide useful role models for young minority group members. They would also serve to expose both whites and minorities to learning and working situations that could help break down barriers between the races.

Between these two opposed views of affirmative action lay a middle position. Supporters of this position agreed that setting aside a fixed number of places for minorities in education or employment did discriminate against whites. They believed, however, that it was permissible to consider minority group membership as a positive quality in deciding who would be admitted to a school or hired for a job. This would be similar to giving consideration to the athletic skills of prospective college students or the ability to "get along" of job applicants. Such factors were often taken into account in making choices among applicants. In the same way, minority group membership could be considered a "plus" in an applicant's favor without the necessity of establishing fixed racial quotas.

All those who had differing viewpoints on affirmative action eagerly awaited the decision of the United States Supreme Court in the case of *Regents of the University of California* v. *Bakke.* The interest and controversy that the case had aroused was indicated by the record number of *amicus curiae* (friend of the court) briefs that had been filed concerning it. These briefs — 61 in all — had been submitted to the Court by organizations or persons who were not actually involved in the Bakke case but who wanted to express an opinion on it. When the case was argued before the Supreme Court on October 12, 1977, the courtroom was packed. Appearing on behalf of the University of California was Archibald Cox, a former solicitor general of the United States who was famous for having been fired as the Watergate special prosecutor in the "Saturday Night Massacre" carried out by Richard

A demonstration in Washington, D.C., calling for a Supreme Court decision against Allan Bakke's admission to the University of California medical school. The Court building can be seen in the background.

Nixon in October 1973. Cox began his argument to the Court by saying,

There is no racially blind method of selection which will enroll today more than a trickle of minority students in the nation's colleges and professions. The suggested alternatives such as helping the "disadvantaged" won't work.

Justice Potter Stewart questioned Cox closely about the matter of quotas:

110

Cox: I want to emphasize the designation of 16 places was not a quota.

Stewart: It did put a limit on the number of white people didn't it?

Cox: . . . It was not pointing a finger at a group which had been marked as inferior in any sense; . . . it was undifferentiated and not stigmatizing . . . .

When Cox had finished, it was the turn of Allan Bakke's lawyer, Reynold H. Colvin of San Francisco. Colvin began his argument by pointing out that he was interested in securing admission to medical school for his client, not in writing law review articles. It quickly became clear, however, that the Court wanted him to argue the constitutional issues:

White: Part of your submission is: even if there are compelling interests, even if there is no alternative, the use of the racial classification is unconstitutional?

Colvin: We believe it is unconstitutional. We do.

Burger: Because it is limited rigidly to 16?

Colvin: No, not because it is limited to 16 but because the concept of race itself as a classification becomes in our history and in our understanding an unjust and improper basis upon which to judge people.

It was not until eight and a half months later that the Supreme Court announced its decision on the Bakke case. This time the courtroom was half-empty when the chief justice led the other eight members of the Court into

Young blacks look on as Reynold H. Colvin, Bakke's lawyer, leaves the Supreme Court Building.

the courtroom at 10:01 A.M. on Wednesday, June 28, 1978. As is the practice of the United States Supreme Court, no prior announcement was made before a decision on the case was reported. The only clue that this day might be somewhat special was the presence in the audience of the wives of several of the justices, who usually attended only when an important decision was to be announced. After Justice Stewart reported the Court's decision in a matter involving pension benefits and Chief Justice Burger dealt with another routine matter, Case No. 76 811, *Regents of the University of California* v. *Bakke,* was announced. Justice Lewis F. Powell, Jr., a courtly Virginia lawyer who had been appointed by President Nixon in 1971, gave the opinion of the Court. He began:

> Perhaps no case in my memory had so much media coverage. We speak today with a notable lack of unanimity. I will try to explain how we divided. It may not be self-evident.

Justice Powell then reported that, by a five-to-four vote, the Court had decided that Allan Bakke was entitled to be admitted to the University of California medical school. Powell explained this part of the decision by saying,

> The guarantee of equal protection cannot mean one thing when applied to one individual and something else when applied to a person of another color. If both are not accorded the same protection, then it is not equal.

Interestingly, though Justice Powell's opinion was officially the opinion of the Court, he was the only one of

Lewis F. Powell gave the opinion of the court in the Bakke case.

its nine members who reached the conclusion that the "equal protection clause" of the 14th Amendment had been violated by the University of California. Justice Powell did *not* think that Title VI of the Civil Rights Act had been violated because the law was designed to deal with discrimination against minorities, not whites. The other four members of the Court who joined Justice Powell in making up a majority on the question of Bakke's admission — Berger, Stevens, Rehnquist, and Stewart — did not agree that Title VI was solely for the benefit of minority group members. They felt that this statute did apply in the Bakke case and that, in Justice Stevens' words, it "required a colorblind standard on the part of government. . . . As succinctly phrased during the Senate debate, under Title VI it is not permissible to say 'yes' to one person, but to say 'no' to another person, only because of the color of his skin." The Stevens group refused to deal with the question of whether the university's actions had violated the 14th Amendment of the Constitution. The four justices said that they had arrived at a decision based solely on Title VI and that the Court's "settled practice is to avoid the decision of a constitutional issue if a case can be fairly decided on statutory ground."

Despite the justices' disagreements on issues, the decision of the Court was clear. A slim five-person majority had decided that Allan Bakke should be admitted to the University of California medical school.

But the larger question of affirmative action itself remained to be settled. In this part of the complicated split decision, Justice Powell joined with the remaining four members of the Court — Brennan, White, Marshall, and Blackmun — in voting to uphold affirmative action. Powell argued that, while rigid numerical quotas based on race alone were in violation of the Constitution, universities did have a legitimate interest in developing a student body made up of a variety of individuals. In achieving this goal, race could be taken into account as a "plus" in admissions decisions when it was considered along with other factors such as geographic diversity, ". . . personal talents, unique work or service experience, leadership potential, maturity, demonstrated compassion, a history of overcoming disadvantage, ability to communicate with the poor, or other qualifications deemed important." According to Powell, affirmative action programs based on this principle were in accordance with the Constitution.

The four members of the Court who agreed with Justice

In the complicated Bakke decision, Justice William Brennan voted with the majority of the Supreme Court in upholding affirmative action and with the minority in approving rigid quota systems.

Powell on the constitutionality of affirmative action would have gone much farther than he in approving programs that gave special preference to minorities. While Powell felt that the Davis program was unconstitutional, a four-member bloc led by Justice Brennan would have upheld the Davis program. These justices believed that "Davis' special admissions program cannot be said to violate the

Constitution simply because it has set aside a predetermined number of places for qualified minority applicants rather than using minority status as a positive factor."

Because Justice Powell voted *against* the Brennan position, along with justices Burger, Stevens, Rehnquist, and Stewart, rigid quotas such as those used at Davis were declared illegal. But because Powell voted *with* Brennan, White, Marshall, and Blackmun on the general issue of affirmative action, approval was given to programs that consider membership in a minority group as a "plus" factor. As in the decision to admit Allan Bakke to medical school, the Supreme Court's decision to uphold affirmative action was made by a small majority of five justices who agreed upon the conclusion but differed on the reasons for that conclusion.

In summary, the decision of the Supreme Court in the Bakke case was divided in this way:

	Admission of Bakke	Constitutionality of Quotas	Constitutionality of Affirmative Action
Blackmun	NO	YES	YES
Brennan	NO	YES	YES
Marshall	NO	YES	YES
White	NO	YES	YES
Powell	*YES*	*NO*	*YES*
Burger	YES	NO	*
Rehnquist	YES	NO	*
Stevens	YES	NO	*
Stewart	YES	NO	*
	YES 5	YES 4	YES 5
	NO 4	NO 5	* 4

*Four justices claimed that the question of whether race could ever be considered a factor in admissions was not an issue in the Bakke case.

Public reaction to the Bakke case was swift and, like the decision itself, reflected a result that showed no clear winners or losers among the supporters and opponents of affirmative action. Critics of affirmative action claimed that the Supreme Court was permitting a policy of race consciousness to be pursued indirectly while forbidding it directly. Nevertheless, they were glad to see Allan Bakke admitted to medical school and rigid quotas abolished. Supporters of affirmative action felt that the admission of Bakke and the striking down of quotas indicated a sharp change in the Supreme Court's position on civil rights. These people feared that the Bakke decision would limit further gains in the area of civil rights, but they were pleased that the concept of affirmative action had at least been upheld. Most observers agreed that many more decisions would probably have to be made by the Supreme Court before the total meaning of the Bakke case would be clear.

And what of Allan Bakke himself? His response to his victory was typical. He smiled slightly on hearing the news and then once again ducked away from reporters. A quiet and private man, Allan Bakke kept his true feelings very much to himself.

Index

120